SOCIAL WORK
THE UNLOVED PROFESSION

New Viewpoints
A Division of Franklin Watts
New York | London

WILLARD C. RICHAN
ALLAN R. MENDELSOHN

SOCIAL WORK THE UNLOVED PROFESSION

Cover by Nicholas Krenitsky

Library of Congress Cataloging in Publication Data

Richan, Willard C
Social work.

Bibliography: p.
1. Social work as a profession.
I. Mendelsohn, Allan R., joint author. II. Title.
HV10.5.R5 361'.0023 73-1267
ISBN 0-531-05350-4
ISBN 0-531-05550-7 (pbk.)

Printed in the
United States of America
6 5 4 3

These are difficult times for the social worker. This is a book about that ubiquitous, burrowing person, a book that deals with a profession so many of us take for granted and so few understand, a book that tackles head-on the crisis overwhelming social work today. These pages tell in the frankest way why the social worker is what he is right now: overdependent, insecure—and unloved.

It is an unusual book. Its authors, each with solid academic and practical experience behind him, agree wholeheartedly on the nature of the crisis that besets their profession and on the absolute necessity for social workers to face up to it. Sections 1 and 4 reflect this agreement.

They disagree on the remedy, however. One author, Allan R. Mendelsohn, believes that only a radical restructuring of social work from its educational base right through to its practice arena in the community will save it from oblivion. In Section 2 he departs from his coauthor and goes his own way, setting forth a radical critique of the "helping" profession and a radical prescription for its future.

In Section 3, Dr. Willard C. Richan goes *his* own way to make the case for reform from within, for a "new professionalism" that will redeem the social worker in the eyes of the surrounding community (especially in the eyes of the poor) and turn him into a positive agent for social change. Signs that this is already happening are, in fact, perceived by Dr. Richan, who underlines the profound significance of his evidence.

In the end, both authors come back to the main focus of the book: social work is a profession in desperate trouble. What matters to both authors is that it be saved because, they say (each in his own way), it is a profession worth saving—almost in spite of itself.

Clifford Solway, Executive Editor, New Viewpoints

CONTENTS

SOCIAL WORK
THE UNLOVED PROFESSION

SECTION I
THE CRISIS

He pauses on the landing to catch his breath. The stairway is black, dark with the acrid smell of dried urine and wood-rot—the sweet and pungent smell of the ghetto tenement. Wearily he climbs the fifth and final flight. The door is unmarked, anonymous. He knocks. A wary eye regards him through the widening crack in the door. He smiles brightly. . . . "Hi—the social worker!" After a pause she lets him in.

She is an emaciated black lady aged far beyond her chronological years. She has two young children and no man in the house. There is no joy in the children's faces as they watch him come in, even though this should be the age of joy for all children. Not even curiosity; their eyes are listless. The woman has recently arrived in the big city from the rural South. She speaks softly in an argot that the worker has trouble understanding. He bends toward her to catch her sounds. The children's bellies are bloated—not from hunger but from eating only starches. She feeds them only rice and potatoes, as she cannot afford to buy meat and vegetables. She knows little about vitamins and minerals, but she does know that her children are sick. She is afraid to take them to a hospital because people die in hospitals. She is frightened that her children will be taken from her.

The two windows in the room are shadeless, but the sun can't penetrate the grime on the panes so the room is dark gray. The naked light bulb doesn't help. She has no one—only a brother who visits her when he is drunk, beats her up, and abuses the children. Neighbors have petitioned a social work agency for help.

The woman is sitting on a rickety kitchen chair. One of the legs is loose, and it wobbles beneath her slight weight. The children stand behind her, afraid to leave. Roaches crawl on the wall. She beats them listlessly with a shoe from time to time, but they continue to creep along. Sometimes they fall from the ceiling, onto the table or into her lap. Rat feces are piled in the corner. The woman's eyes are downcast. She cannot bring herself to look up and meet the social worker's eyes.

A terrible sense of impotence envelops the social worker. "How can I help you, lady? For God's sake, where do I even start? How can I feed and clothe and rehouse you, so that maybe you and your children can live with some dignity? Shall I take your children from you so that maybe they will have some slight chance to survive? Shall I try to keep you together so that you will have at least a sense of family in your misery? I can get you some food, of course, but just enough to keep you alive. There is no bounding good health in sight for you or your children. I can get you some money for clothes, but it won't be enough; they'll be cheap and soon they, too, will be rags. I can rehouse you, but only with new rats and other roaches. I'm a social worker, lady. I've spent a few years in social work school. What the hell have I got to offer you? Where the hell do I begin? What the hell do all my learned theories have to do with you and your kids . . . and this filthy place you live in . . . and this terrible tenement . . . and this godawful ghetto? I don't know, lady . . . I just don't know. Look, I can makeshift for you, lady. I'll put a patch here and a patch there. I'll try. I'm sorry . . . I have other people to see, lady. Some are even worse off than you are. Maybe some of them can use what help I have to offer . . . maybe. I'm sorry, lady. . . ."

CHAPTER 1
THE UNLOVED PROFESSION

We use all the money that comes to us from subscriptions solely for salaries and other matters of administration, and we believe that money so used intelligently confers more benefit on the poor than money given for material relief. Material relief is a dangerous remedy....

—From a treatise on the training of charity workers, 1903.

The client in the foregoing encounter does not necesarily represent all people on welfare, many of whom show an amazing resilience in the face of overwhelming odds. What it does typify is the exercise in mutual frustration that so often occurs between the bewildered client—the victim of an unjust social order—and the equally bewildered social worker, who struggles with his own entrapment in the oppressive system. One wonders how long this worker will continue the struggle before he, too, capitulates and flees to the protective environment of a private agency tucked away in some comfortable suburban enclave. Once upon a time social workers mainly served the poor, but the more "professional" the field has become, the more its members have disengaged themselves from the grimy problems of poverty, discrimination, and urban decay.

It is ironic, for the existence of the social work profession can best be justified by the continuing presence of the poor in a society, and the poor are what social work purports to be all about. It may come as a considerable surprise to some that social work—with its emphasis on the development of knowledge and skills in dealing with social problems, with its highly organized agencies for the delivery of needed services —*has so very little to do with the poor today.*

Social work came about in the first place because of

the presence of the poor. It grew out of humanistic concerns and religious principles and attempted to give at least something to the wretched. Its service was limited and fragmented—scarcely up to what today would be considered minimal standards—but the hungry *did* receive some food, some shelter, and some clothing. Social work has since evolved into a planned scientific intervention into the lives of people. Its rhetoric, its many statements of purpose, its professional code of ethics—all of its public pronouncements continue to reflect a deep and overriding concern for the poor. Yet for all its sophistication and expertise, today's social work still can only offer today's poor *some* food, *some* shelter, *some* clothing—if it offers them anything at all. Most social workers have directed their energy and interest elsewhere.[1]

It is as if the problem of poverty has been overcome, as if the poor of our society have been wiped from the face of the earth by some fabulous beneficent act and as if social work, its major task accomplished, could now afford the luxury of practice with the less needy and the less hungry. As a matter of fact, if the poor were to vanish suddenly from the cities and countryside of America, there would be almost no change in either the teaching or the practice of social work as it is presently carried out. Social work would continue to be what it is for the simple reason that its expertise is directed primarily not toward solving the gritty problems of poverty, but toward soothing the emotional hangups of the middle class. Social workers have long since abandoned the arid ground of poverty for greener pastures. Something very significant happened to that initial humanism that inspired and helped social work to develop into a "professional" service.

Like every generalization, this one is only partly true. Of all graduate social work students in 1966, for example, one out of every seven planned to enter the field of public assistance upon graduating, and roughly half intended to work in some kind of public agency.[2] However, this probably reflects the fact that governmental stipends—with a requirement that the recipient return to the public agency to work after graduation—are the major way in which social work students finance their education. Overall, only about 7 percent of all graduate social workers are employed in public assistance, most of them in supervisory and administrative positions where they do not deal directly with the poor. Many graduate social workers are employed in other public agencies which also serve poor people, most notably in the field of child welfare. But again the professionals gravitate to jobs up the hierarchical ladder where they can deal with the poor at arm's length, through intermediaries.[3]

While the first social worker brought his hungry client a basketful of food, his counterpart today may bear only a psychoanalytic glossary (if he even appears at all). As the requirements for social work practice become more exacting and more oriented to specialized expertise, less of this expertise reaches the poor. This is as true of social work as it is of the other specialized services offered in our society. The longer the time spent in the training of a specialist, the higher the price of his service. It follows that the higher the price, the farther removed it is from the reach of the poor.

Even though social work's stock-in-trade is communication, it has not yet developed the tools to reach the poor. Social work has not only *not* been able to communicate with the poor, its willingness to do so has been weak and haphazard. The instruments of help that the social worker has to offer are too abstract and intellectual. They are designed for a client population that is attuned to middle-class values. They have evolved from a training system that is focused upon teaching abstract concepts, abetting upward aspirations, and resolving neurotic conflicts. These helping devices have very little meaning to people who are hungry and ghettoized. Do they have nothing at all to contribute to people whose lives are walled in despair?

The distance between the givers and the receivers of service is increasing daily, particularly so in view of social work's drive toward increased specialization. For their own part, the poor experience growing frustration, and with this comes a growing reliance on direct political action to get what they need. The strategies of the poor have, in fact, become more and more foreign to the archeological diggers in the ruins of the middle-class family structure.

To the social worker, the poor have dwindled away not in size but in presence. They have ceased to be sweating and struggling human beings, real to the senses. For the social worker, they have been transformed into abstract entities to be studied from a distance. Even when the social work agency is physically located in a ghetto, the gap between the givers and receivers of service can be so immense that it would make little difference if one party were on the moon.

There is a social work agency located in a sprawling horror in Brooklyn, New York, which offers psychoanalytic services to a population reeling under the impact of crime, slums, rats, and despair. Precious few of the residents of this ghetto are "motivated" to seek this kind of service. Of these, only a small proportion actually receive psychotherapeutic support from the social worker. These select few are seen individually for the traditional psychoanalytic hour; obviously, very few people can be seen. There are psychiatrists on staff who also offer psychoanalytic hours—not to the population—but to the social workers! This agency and its services are as remote from their community as if they were located in the Himalayas.

If this particular agency were an exception in the practice of social work in the United States today, its practice might be experimentally justified. Since this agency is closer to the *norm* of professional practice, however, and since this example may be multiplied a hundredfold, then legitimate questions concerning the nature and function of social work practice today should be raised.

Not only has the distance between the worker and the client progressively increased with the specialization of the profession; it has also become quite obvious that the poor themselves are being systematically excluded from the ranks of the professional workers. Recently one graduate school of social work arranged tours of the ghettos for its first-year students. This was so that the students would have some idea of what being poor meant, of what the poor looked like, of how they dressed and how they lived!

Graduates of schools of social work do not gravitate easily toward working with the poor. Following graduation they tend to cluster around the private agencies where therapeutic services are being offered to the middle class, rather than join the public agencies that have assumed the burden of dealing directly with the poor. And why not? It is those private agencies where the tools that social workers have been taught to use can be used. As for the poor, they fall into a limbo—the "unmotivated," the "hostile" client, unloved and unserved, unsuitable for the social worker's ministrations.

At the same time, the poor have become increasingly disenchanted with the social worker. The clichés of social work sound with greater hollowness as poverty continues to grow and as the gap between the unmet needs of the poor and the opulence of the middle class becomes more obvious. The complaints of the poor about the lack of service, about the lack of understanding of what their needs actually are, and about the paternalistic rhetoric of the rest of society and its failure to deliver on it grow increasingly bitter. Frustration has turned to anger, and the poor no longer seek the help of the social worker. They have closed the door of the ghetto in his face and have even denied him access to its streets. The poor are convinced that whatever help they may hope to get will not come from the social worker. It will come from themselves—out of their rage and violence, their self-help strategies, their political organizations, and the radical stances of the dispossessed around the world. It will *not* come from the social worker's identification of early toilet-training problems as the root cause of poverty! [4]

Looking ahead, the poor have come to expect even less help from their historic friend, the social worker. They read the handwriting on the wall as spelling more psychotherapy, more specialization, closer identification with middle-class problems, less concern for the delivery of services to the ghetto, and, most important, no discernible efforts to solve those conditions that produce poverty in the first place.

Not only are the poor angry and frustrated and the ghettos, plagued with crime, turning our cities into armed camps; other related social issues impinge upon the social work profession: a generation of youth in rebellion, drug abuse, civil disobedience, rising crime rates, revolutionary rumblings in minority groups, terror in the streets, the fouling of the environment, starvation in Appalachia, dying urban centers, blighted rural areas, widespread unemployment, muggings, bombings, corruption, political disenfranchisement, sickness and disease—the list grows daily.

Where is social work in all of this? Social work cannot be expected to resolve urgent social problems by itself, but it would not be unreasonable to expect that the "helping" profession would be significantly involved with them. Yet the voice of social worker is painfully absent from the councils attempting to deal with these issues. The absence *is* painful, because it must bitterly remind the social worker of his functioning inadequacy. It must remind him of the huge disparity between what he expected social work to train him to do, what social work promised it would train him to do, and what social work has *actually* trained him to do. *The fact of the matter is that by and large social workers are not trained to deal with social problems directly, at the point where basic social forces create them. Instead, social workers are taught to engage in continual mop-up operations . . . the sanitation department of society.*

What *are* social workers trained to do? Mainly, to resolve the problems of middle-class families in suburbia. And while the middle-class family in suburbia may have its problems, these problems are not the most pressing ones of contemporary society. The question to be asked, then, is why does social work have so little to say on the important social issues of the day? Whatever happened to social work?

And yet there is something audacious in the concept of a profession whose *sole* reason for existence is to respond to human need, *whatever* its shape and substance. Every other profession has carefully defined boundaries to its domain—boundaries that serve the dual purpose of delineating the scope of its members' responsibility and of protecting the professional "turf" against interlopers. Social work's breadth is at once its genius and its undoing. In intent, it is the clearest expression of man's humanity toward his fellow man. But its lack of clear boundaries, and thereby the inability to establish exclusive claim to any territory, has shot social work through and through with anxiety about its identity and worth.

Social workers seldom openly acknowledge this insecurity, but they bear the indelible marks of an institution convinced of its own failure. Seeking to do good, social workers are told that they destroy and dehumanize and desert the very people they wish to serve. Seeking professional status, they are second-class citizens in the ranks of the professions. Obsessively pragmatic, they cannot point to any tangible results in the society around them. Having no less than the full range of man's ills as their chosen turf, they settle for the narrow slice of the action allowed them by their agencies.

And social workers secretly know that it is all true—that they have never really achieved what they set out to achieve. They show it, too, in their preoccupation with their public image, in the sweeping claims in their propaganda, and in their sudden inarticulateness when they are asked what they do or when they hear their profession and their clients criticized.

But then the paradox: for a profession nobody loves, social work has been strangely sought after. For many years the demand and the funded job slots ran far ahead of the supply. The simplest explanation for this popularity of the unloved and unpopular is the apparently insatiable American appetite for services of all kinds, including social services. The poor and other captive populations serve a very important function in all this: they provide the necessary excuse for this society, plagued as it is by the ghosts of its puritanical past, to indulge itself with social amenities. There is a regular sequence in which social services, supposedly introduced to meet the urgent needs of the poor and other social victims, turn out in reality to be provisions for the majority who are *not* poor.

Social Security payments became a right—*except* for the very poor. Child-guidance services, having originated as an answer to the problem of juvenile delinquency, became an expensive form of therapy for children of affluence. Housing and urban renewal programs, founded as the salvation of the slum-dweller, have turned to destroy their assumed beneficiaries while reaping vast benefits for commercial interests. The list goes on and on. As social services have followed this familiar pattern, professional social workers—hungry for the respectability that comes with affluent clientele—also have disengaged from the poor they claim as their special concern.

The demand for social workers has another, less obvious, explanation: the need to avert social disorder and manage the behavior of potentially embarrassing segments of the population. For years social workers have spread among America's poor the gospel that their misery is their own fault and not that of the system. This practice of "blaming the victim" may be cast in more or less harsh terms, but its consistency throughout the history of social work is striking. In 1892, the message was stated with unabashed candor:

> The moment it is understood by the idle and shiftless in a community, such as we find in one of our modern cities, that they can, on the ground of destitution, claim a certain amount of support while still remaining at large and enjoying the sweets of liberty, the door is opened to a perfect flood of pauperism and consequent vice.[5]

Compare that with this reference to so-called multi-problem families in a 1961 issue of *Social Work,* the journal of the National Association of Social Workers:

Primitive in ego development, they are quickly overwhelmed by outside pressures and anxieties of the moment, and seek the worker out in their pain and panic. . . . Over and over again one senses, beneath a hostile veneer, an oral character; a client who never stops demanding. . . . The dependency is pervasive and the client sucks from neighbors, shopkeepers, bartenders, and news vendors as well as family members and social workers.[6]

By means of such labeling, together with their own special blend of sympathy and sternness, social workers have helped pacify the seething heart of the nation's slums. The dedicated practitioners who have labored in the ghettos and in the massive public agencies through the years, while their colleagues escaped to greener fields, have not set out intentionally to keep the lid on in behalf of the status quo. Indeed, they are shocked by the suggestion that this is their true mission.

But social workers are employees. They carry out assignments given them by their bureaucratic masters. The social welfare industry—that conglomeration of governmental and voluntary agencies providing social services—has a very clear function of keeping the poor and disenfranchised from causing trouble.

This is a book about social work, a profession that nursed heroic aspirations and wanted to make a real difference in the human condition. Somewhere along the way it ran off course. It became unsure of its direction and ensnared in bureaucratic red tape, the captive of welfare institutions that cared more about their own survival than the people they were intended to serve.

Or had social work always been the flunky of the social welfare industry and a victim of its own obsession with professional prestige? Had the heroic aims been only an illusion—a way for social workers to persuade themselves and others that they were capable of something better?

This is a profession that, as it seeks to free itself from bureaucratic bondage and realize some part of its high purpose, is now being forced to come to terms with its own limitations.

Social work has become the unloved profession—unloved by its clients whom it has ceased to serve, unloved by the system that it has failed to reinforce, unloved by its peers whose respect it has lost, and, most poignantly, since it has not remained true to its own commitments, unloved even by itself.

CHAPTER 2
THE ELUSIVE PARAMETERS OF THE SOCIAL WORK PROFESSION

Social work is based on humanitarian, democratic ideals. Professional social workers are dedicated to service for the welfare of mankind; to the disciplined use of a recognized body of knowledge about human beings and their interactions; and to the marshaling of community resources to promote the well-being of all without discrimination.

Opening statement of the Code of Ethics of the National Association of Social Workers.

Well, what is social work all about? To answer this, it may be best first of all to take a look at the arena in which social workers operate. At first glance it is surprising to discover that the arena is so wide and varied in size and depth. Social workers are all over the society; they turn up everywhere. Some are self-employed, engaged in private practice, but the bulk of them are employed in private or public agencies. You meet social workers in schools, hospitals, welfare departments, correctional institutions, residential treatment settings, settlement houses, mental health settings, adoption agencies, community service organizations, veterans' bureaus, the military, nursing homes, and children's services. They work in courts, prisons, in literally all types of service agencies; they are even found tucked away in private industry. Social workers populate government bureaus and the civil service at every level; many are involved in social work education as well.

In short, social workers are ubiquitous and at every level of society, performing every role from worker to top management. They serve in "host" agencies, such as hospitals, which are dominated by another profession. Sometimes they are an entire agency in themselves. Their specific tasks are as diverse as the places in which they work. In one setting the social worker may be enrolling a disabled person in a rehabilitation program; in another, arranging for the adoption of a child. Or he may be organizing an activity program for children in an institution, administering a complex welfare service, drawing up a strategy for a mental health clinic, or doing a stint of marital counseling on behalf of a troubled couple. A few social workers are helping people organize to make demands on the system.

What is it that binds together all these people doing such different jobs in varied settings? The link is that they are all members of a practice field. Social work by its very nature is operational. It has a pragmatic and specific function: the provision of service to people who need service. While there are many differences as to how and to whom the service should be provided, the basic purpose of the field and the justification for its entire being lie in the delivery of services to the people who are in need of help. If people's needs are not being met, then the "welfare of mankind" is not being promoted and social work is not fulfilling its stated purpose. This is a simple but usually overlooked fact about the nature of the profession.

While social work has many individual distinctions, it has one in particular that sets it apart from its fellow professions. Social work is the only field of practice that envisions itself as dealing with man in his entirety. No other field of practice even presumes to make this claim. But while social work claims to deal with the whole man—social, economic, physical, emotional, and cultural—in actuality its predominant practice patterns have focused narrowly on the psychological.

Likewise, while social work calls itself an eclectic field—drawing its knowledge-base from a vast range of scientific disciplines—through most of its history its real theoretical underpinnings have been almost totally psychoanalytic. These two paradoxes—the reputed vastness and the real narrowness—are related. For Freudian theory led social workers to limit their practice to areas where its principles had the greatest relevance.

In addition to being an area of practice and a means of delivering services, social work stands for a system of values. Its basic stance is humanistic, with emphasis on democratic principles and processes. Simply stated, the role of the social worker is to *"help people to help themselves."* Although this phrase is open to a range of interpretations, its best sense implies opening up areas of choice for people, giving them access to those choices, helping them to develop and explore their potential for living. The social worker neither dictates nor directs. He enables. He enables people to survive according to their own needs and desires.

Self-determination is perhaps the most significant principle involved here. Self-determination implies the right of people to make their own choices, regardless of whether such choices are considered appropriate or inappropriate or whether they are deemed good or bad by others. While self-determination is a relatively easy principle to subscribe to in theory, it is an extremely difficult one to put into practice. One would not expect, for example, a four-year-old child to make basic decisions concerning his existence. The social worker will listen to and be aware of the child's needs and wants, but a decision about whether this child remains with his alcoholic mother or is moved to another home environment is not the child's to make. Nor would a social worker stand by while a severely disturbed person took his own or another's life.

There are other situations in which self-determination must in all good sense yield to, or at least be modified by, individual circumstances. The "art" of social work—and social work must be considered more an art than a science—lies in determining a strategy of intervention that leaves the individual with the most freedom of choice possible in a very real sense.

Social work also represents a fundamental belief in the *dignity* of man and in his inherent worth, whatever his social situation, his race, his color, or his life style. Again, more easily stated than accomplished. Social workers, after all, are human beings, with their own share of prejudices and negative feelings about people. The art of social work involves learning to handle these feelings when dealing with people.

This is one of the most difficult and painful parts of the whole business of social work; ironically so, since the social worker usually has such a strong personal commitment to his work. The skilled social worker learns to keep the influence of his personal prejudices to a minimum. At the very least he recognizes them. His fundamental concern is and must be the world—not his own private world—but the world of the people he is serving. In order to relate to the world of others, he must have some understanding of, and ability to control, his own world. A large degree of *self-awareness* can permit the social worker to perform objectively and with the utmost respect for the dignity of the persons with whom he is dealing.

Another principle to which social workers subscribe—in theory at least—is that of *confidentiality.* Confidentiality is one of the most sensitive aspects of the profession; consequently, there is a growing tendency to shy away from it rather than face it openly. Confidentiality represents the individual's right to privacy. The relationship between the social worker and the client is based on trust. Clients are asked to share their feelings, thoughts, and problems freely with either the open or the implicit assumption that the exchange will be "confidential."

But social workers are trained in and have great faith

in the keeping of records, and transactions between themselves and their clients invariably find their way into the "record." Since most social workers work in agencies, record-keeping is an essential part of their accountability to the agency which employs them. The confidential material is thus available to supervisors, to other agency staff, to agency administration, and at times to sources *outside* the agency—the judicial system, for example. Social workers are often in a quandary as to what information they should commit to the records, and they must often evaluate how a particular agency may use—or abuse—the material. On the other hand, they must subscribe to agency requirements for the faithful transcription of their own work. Social workers are thus both responsible to their clients and accountable to their agencies.

While it is extremely difficult to protect the confidentiality of information in private agencies, it is still more difficult in public agencies. There is no such thing as privileged communication in social work. Unlike doctors, lawyers, and clergymen, a social worker who refuses to disclose his client's personal business is subject to contempt of court and could even be sent to jail. In public agencies, of course, public funds are involved, and the public is far more sensitive to protection of its tax money than to protection of the dignity and privacy of welfare clients. Should the social worker report to his welfare agency that his client has a part-time job that enables her to buy just a little more food than her survival budget allows? Or should his ears and eyes be shut with a silent prayer that no one else will turn the client in?

This conflict between responsibility toward the client and accountability for public funds can assume frightening proportions and, at times, tear the social worker apart. His professional ethics on the one side, the majesty of the law on the other—the social worker's position is not an enviable one. Legitimate questions may be raised as to whether a social worker can ethically assume investigative functions in verifying facts for agencies or in determining the eligibility of a client for public assistance, particularly when the laws governing the issuance of monies for welfare are strikingly inhumane, unjust, and exceedingly punitive. Social workers are used as investigators, and it may take some lengthy exercises in self-justification to square this with the social worker's professional code of ethics. This is one reason why social workers are often loath to work in public agencies.

For several decades now social work practice has been broken down into three major areas. The first, the oldest and the most familiar, is casework. The focus of casework is on the individual or the nuclear family group. The caseworker functions on the basis of a one-to-one relationship with the person in need of service. There is an interactive flow between client and worker. Casework is still the largest area of concentration in schools of social work. It is what most social workers are prepared to practice when they receive their graduate degrees in social work. (See Table 1).

In the early years of the twentieth century, caseworkers tended to be identified by the fields in which they practiced: they were psychiatric social workers, or medical social workers, or school social workers, or charity workers. The fragmentation was reflected in their education and their separate professional associations. Eventually the distinctions among caseworkers lessened, although it is still hard for caseworkers with experience, say, in child welfare, to move into the more prestigious psychiatric agencies.

Group work involves work with several clients at the

Table 1
Area Concentration for Master's Degree Students enrolled in Accredited Graduate Schools of Social Work in the United States and Canada, by Method Concentration—November, 1970 *

Casework	4,814
Group work	1,081
Community organization	1,245
Casework community organization or group work	2,303
Group work community organization	56
Administration	277
Research	45
Social work practice (generic)	2,746
Other or none	934

* Representing seventy accredited schools of social work in the United States, and four in Canada.

same time. Here the interactive flow is both between worker and client and between client and client. In essence the client is a number of individuals, and the group itself is an important ingredient in the work that is to be done. The social worker enhances the flow between members and the work of the group as a whole but traditionally has avoided becoming the group leader as such, the theory being that the group should develop its own leadership.

During the 1930's, group work became an accepted component of social work education and practice. The stereotype was a person who led group activities in a neighborhood center. But more social group work graduates took administrative jobs and spent less and less time leading groups. Social group workers were constantly hounded by their sense of being second-class citizens in a second-class profession. Lacking the prestige of the caseworkers, increasing numbers of group workers abandoned community agencies and moved to psychiatric and rehabilitational settings.

Social group work never really recovered from this personality split. One element gravitated to clinical settings, where they found caseworkers who were finding the one-to-one relationship too restrictive and welcomed the added breadth that groups provided. The other element in group work, which retained a basic loyalty to the social settlement spirit, moved increasingly to community action and organization and planning.

The third major social work method is community organization. Because of the relative newness of community organization training in social work education, many of the social workers practicing in this field were trained as caseworkers or group workers. The ferment of the 1960's both gave major impetus to this social work specialty and heightened the dilemmas surrounding it.

The explosion of federally subsidized community programs drastically raised the demand for social workers who could practice on a community level. But traditional community organization was closely identified with health and welfare councils, the symbol of social welfare's irrelevance to the rising tempo of urban discontent and established voluntary agencies' stubborn insistence that private philanthropy was somehow superior to governmental provision.

Yet of all branches of social work, community organization has historically been the most pragmatic and the least shackled by ideological niceties. When the social welfare industry needed public apologists and fund-raisers, community organizers responded to the demand. When the ferment of the 1960's called for a shift in priorities, community organizers found it easier to adapt than did caseworkers. And as planning, managerial, and research capability gained favor in the 1970's, community organization was the sector of social work practice and education toward which social welfare systems turned.

Despite what appear to be major differences among these three areas of concentration, there is more similarity and overlap in technique and practice than is apparent at first glance. That their differences rather than their similarities have been emphasized in professional schools has meant an unfortunate fragmentation of the social work profession. "Old line" agencies geared to traditional casework have trouble accepting a group work approach, even when the needs of their client population dictate this as the most effective way to render service. To illustrate, some casework agencies will even refuse to see members of the same family at one time, although they see presented problems as rooted in family malfunctioning, and the effects of those problems are felt by all members. The rationale for this refusal is the notion that seeing the whole family together would violate the sanctity of the one-to-one relationship or destroy confidentiality. Granted that this narrow approach is now more the exception than the rule, it still remains too prevalent to be dismissed lightly. "Seeing" the family often represents a token acknowledgment of the new wave, but the significant work may still remain in the one-to-one casework method.

For many established social workers, group work is still perceived as an alien technique, one requiring the development of a whole new set of skills that inevitably sets it apart from the rest of the profession. The resistance to such a mild modification of established practice speaks volumes about social workers' innate insecurity and the extreme difficulty they have in coming to grips with new ideas or innovative approaches.

We have been describing the three methods that have dominated social work for decades. There seems to be general agreement, however, that the old trilogy of casework, group work, and community organization is on the way out. Dramatic evidence of this is the decline in the percentage of students majoring in casework in graduate programs—from roughly 85 percent a few years ago to 36 percent, according to a spokesman for the Council on Social Work Education.[1] Of course, to some extent this represents a change in terminology, with the same practices being called by new names. The real question is whether the social work profession will reorganize itself in ways that will foster a vital meaningful role for itself, or whether it will allow its shape and substance to be dictated by the internal needs of social welfare bureaucracies.

Social work is practiced today in two distinct contexts. The older and more traditional arena of practice is the *agency*—the bureaucratic agglomeration that offers a range of social services to a range of people. The second arena, a newer arrival on the social work scene, is the private office of the social worker. Here, on a fee-paying basis, the social worker is in business for himself.*

---

* As of 1967 it was estimated that between 3,000 and 4,000 social work professionals from a total 42,000 were private practitioners. That comes out to 7–10 percent. There are now about 55,000 professionals; that could mean 5,000 private practitioners, assuming the ratio continued. *Encyclopedia of Social Work* (New York: National Association of Social Workers, 1971), Vol. 2, p. 952.

If there is a distinction between the psychologist, the psychiatrist, and the social worker in private practice, it lies essentially in the matter of fees—the social worker usually charging the least for his services (even here his innate insecurity dogs him like his own shadow). The psychiatrist may dispense medication and the three disciplines may choose to frame different credentials for their offices, but what they do is, in essence, the same thing. The social worker in private practice *is* a psychotherapist. Despite his denials and his insistence that he places more emphasis on the environmental factors, the fact of the matter remains that his techniques of treatment are the same as those of the psychologist and psychiatrist in private practice.[2]

More important, however, is not what these social workers practice but whom they serve. It is not the masses of the poor, the socially alienated, the disenfranchised—that they serve. *Their* clients (now patients) are drawn from the middle classes. It is only the middle-class who can afford even the lesser fees the social worker in private practice charges. It is entirely conceivable that a social worker in private practice has never worked intimately with a poor person in his whole professional career. It may even be that he never met one during his professional training as well —one can wonder why he is called a social worker at all. Yet the social worker in private practice is considered by many professionals and educators to represent the zenith of a social work career. The social worker as private practitioner is the logical outcome of established social work practice and current educational trends.

Many students go to schools of social work because they offer the least costly means of securing the credentials necessary for admission into advanced schools of psychotherapy. Some schools of social work even encourage students toward this end.

The larger part of social work practice, however, takes place within an agency framework. Agencies are of two kinds, public and private (voluntary, nonprofit). The public agency is, of course, operated as a government service and supported by public funds. The people served by public agencies are by and large at the bottom of the public-misery barrel. When all other resources fail and when the private agencies cannot or will not provide, the last resort before oblivion is the public agency. One of the stark facts about public agencies is that they cannot limit their intake. While private agencies to a very large extent can determine whom they will serve, the public agencies cannot—there is simply no other place for a poor person to go.

Private agencies, sectarian in origin, historically provided a wide range of services in the areas in which social workers selected to work. Their services, in essence, were concrete: they distributed money, food, clothing, shelter, etc. Following the Depression in the 1930's the governmental welfare system assumed an increasing share of these responsibilities. As a result, the voluntary agencies had to develop new definitions of what they were about. Therefore, they incorporated the major breakthroughs in psychology that were occurring at that time into their practice. Psychiatry became the model for social work practice.[3]

While the professional social worker generally has a voice in the operation of the private agencies, basic decision-making and directional thrusts remain in the hands of the boards of directors or trustees. A profile of these boards reveals, along with established authorities in their field, nominal participants, wealthy patricians, people of "liberal" persuasion, and commercially successful entrepreneurs who have risen from humble beginnings.

One study of board composition [4] of voluntary social

agencies across the country demonstrated the essential elitism in their composition:

Businessmen	21.0%
Physicians	15.1
Industrialists	8.8
Wives of businessmen	8.6
Wives of industrialists	5.7
Attorneys	5.2
Educators	4.1
Labor representatives	3.9
Financiers	3.6
Employees of welfare agencies	3.4
Government officials	2.3
Clergy	1.8
Editors and journalists	1.8
Registered nurses	0.8
Others (mainly housewives)	13.8
	100.0%

While these figures were gathered before the spate of concern about participation of the poor and the clients in decision-making that grew out of the urban crisis of the 1960's, there have been few significant changes since then. The inclusion of selected low-income and minority persons on agency boards has been a prime case of tokenism. Not until quite recently has there been any representation on any governing boards of the population that is served. These policy-making bodies, while "liberal" in attitude, are basically conservative and Establishment-oriented in practice. They tend to be uncomfortable with social workers—the "do-gooders"—but will remain steadfastly loyal as long as social work practice remains in the area of psychological intervention. Fundamentally, they understand that a real redistribution of resources and power poses a threat to their vital interests.

To sum up, social work portrays itself today as a humanitarian field of practice devoted to "service for the welfare of mankind," and as an ameliorative field that promises to help cope with some of society's problems. It is positively magnetic in its appeal to the young idealist and the socially concerned, to the would-be reformer. Its methods and techniques are "enabling" tools, neither dictatorial nor authoritarian, but rather designed to open up areas of choice for people to opt for according to their own needs and desires.

Social work's value system is embedded in a code of ethics, one that is democratic, non-discriminatory, and consummately altruistic. It is a system that reflects a profound respect for the dignity of man, his right to self-determination, and his right to privacy as well. These are remarkable values—values well worth subscribing to. They are, moreover, values well worth preserving even if professional social work as conceived and practiced today is consigned to oblivion.

There is often confusion in the mind of the public between "social work," a professional field, and "social welfare," the set of institutions we are calling an industry. Some social workers are employed *outside* of organized social welfare—for instance as consultants to private industry or as private practitioners—and the majority of employees in social welfare institutions are *not* professional social workers. The largest single social welfare program—the Social Security insurance system for the elderly, disabled, and survivors—is run not by social workers but primarily by economists and accountants.

The social welfare industry is large, and it keeps

on growing. It expands regardless of the political and economic views of the individual in the White House or the party with a congressional majority. The governmental funds going into this industry alone account for more than one-seventh of the gross national product, and more and more it is governmental funds that prop up the entire enterprise—public and voluntary.[5]

The private sector of the industry—a complex array of religious and other nonprofit agencies—used to dominate, largely as a consequence of America's historic aversion to "big government." But in recent decades voluntary agencies have come to rely increasingly on tax money—particularly federal funds—for their survival, all the while fighting efforts by politicians to control their programs. Likewise, states and localities have been willing to finance their social welfare activities with federal money, but they have jealously resisted federal encroachment on control of the operations.

The result has been an interesting paradox: the national government has exerted only the weakest kind of authority over the quality, equity, and coverage of the local public and voluntary social services that it has subsidized, but except for a brief flirtation with social action in the 1960's it has dealt harshly with those programs involving social action or challenging existing policies and institutions. The selective way in which government has thus exercised its power makes clear both where its priorities are and what the functions are it ascribes to the social welfare industry.

What are the specific activities of the social welfare industry? First and foremost it dispenses money: $76,000,000,000, including insurance benefits and public assistance, in 1971. More than $6,000,000,000 of that went to children and their families under the controversial Aid to Families with Dependent Children (AFDC) program.[6]

This program is the favorite whipping boy of welfare critics who see it as spawning every imaginable social ill among the poor and the minorities. In most families receiving AFDC, the father is missing from the household. It was inevitable that this program, concentrated as it was among fatherless, low-income families, would from its inception in the mid-1930's be a political target. As population and migration shifts made blacks the most visible part of the AFDC caseload, it encompassed perfectly the American stereotypes linking poverty, race, laziness, and immorality.

While social work professionals have consistently supported governmental provisions for Social Security insurance benefits and public assistance, they have tended to avoid employment in the latter programs.[7] In public assistance programs such as AFDC, the clients are assumed to be in need of rehabilitation and social control; this assumption has become more entrenched as the caseloads in public assistance have become increasingly black.

But while such programs have until recently sought professional social workers, the latter have turned to the more prestigious fields of mental health and family treatment and their more middle-class clientele. Although social workers tend to rate voluntary agencies above public agencies, the auspices are less an issue than the type of program and the type of client. For example, public child welfare services, which have less directly to do with financial need, have had much greater success in recruiting professional social workers than has public assistance—even though they were often under the same public authority. This can be seen clearly in Table 2.

Table 2
Public Assistance and Child Welfare Workers With Two Years or More of Graduate Social Work Education in 1964

	Public Assistance	Public Child Welfare
All positions	4.8%	26.0%
Caseworkers	1.2%	15.0%

Source: *Closing the Gap . . . in Social Work Education and Manpower* (Washington, D.C.: Government Printing Office, 1965), pp. 15f.

Not only are professional social workers more than five times as likely to work in public child welfare as in public assistance; the boundaries between public and voluntary child welfare are often quite open. Thus, a person employed in public child welfare may move into a voluntary agency if governmental regulations and swollen caseloads become overwhelming. On the other hand, there is virtually no private counterpart of public income-maintenance programs. The public assistance worker rarely has any non-governmental alternative within his own field.

It is hard for the mind to encompass the enormous sprawl of the social welfare industry. In addition to money payment programs and child welfare services, it includes social services in hospitals and community health clinics; institutions and services for the mentally ill and retarded; juvenile court services; adult probation and parole; services in the public schools; community recreation programs; community action and development projects; and a wide range of individual and family counseling services. A privately endowed treatment clinic and the huge public assistance bureaucracy have little in common on the surface, but they are both part of the same industry, and both in their idealized self-images are working toward the same goal of human betterment.

While the private agencies have tended to employ the lion's share of social work professionals and to dominate their thinking, the charity dollar is puny beside the resources channeled through governmental welfare programs. In fiscal year 1967–1968, for example, over 84 percent of all welfare outlays in this country were public funds. In 1969, those celebrated symbols of the charitable spirit in America, the Red Feather drives, collected about $816,000,000 for causes ranging from local recreation and counseling agencies to the American Red Cross and the Salvation Army. But public funds going for health services *alone* were more than ten times that amount, and the total public social welfare expenditure excluding education was roughly one hundred times the United Fund total.[8]

To understand social work—its strengths and its weaknesses—it is necessary to grasp its essentially ideological character. More than most professions that claim a scientific technology, social work is as much a set of ends as it is the means for achieving them. So social workers tell themselves and each other and the world of their lofty sentiments, and the layman begins to suspect that there is not much more to the field. Social workers do, in fact, have a technology; perhaps it is more accurate to say technologies because of the diverse specialties that come under the social work rubric. But it is true that the more persistent and enduring elements are ideological, and the shared value system provides virtually the only core around which the diverse elements can unite and claim to be a profession.[9]

Social work is a field that demands total involvement. Many social workers become engrossed virtually all their waking hours in the work they are doing. And why not? Social work is a fascinating occupation: it requires an investment in the life of other people; it deals with combinations of human beings interacting in society; it is intellectually challenging; and it even propounds new dimensions for man living together with his fellows.

Social work is powerfully seductive—so absorbing that its raison d'être is at once a morbid preoccupation and something to be brushed aside as academic and theoretical. The work itself becomes its justification for being. If, for example, one's work relieves internal distress and if relieving internal distress is a worthwhile business, why raise questions as to what one is about? The nagging question, however, persists: Is this really what social work is all about?

Social work's relevancy today is more than an academic debate. It has become a crucial issue not only for itself but also for society at large. As society's problems surge around it, there must be a general accounting of the social work profession. What is it really doing? What contribution does it *really* make? And if it is failing to contribute—*why?*

The passage quoted earlier from the Code of Ethics is not exactly electrifying, although ". . . dedicated to service for the welfare of mankind" may fan a spark in some breasts. At the very least it evokes a humanistic promise. To the young it offers the expectation of a career based on direct involvement in the crucial issues of today's world. In the years since the Peace Corps, VISTA, and the New Frontier, youth seems to have become increasingly distrustful of ambitious humanistic pronouncements. Fortunately, the young can still shudder at the rank injustices of our society—at the poverty, the discrimination, and the callous enslavement of so many—and they can still believe that there must be a better way for men to live together. With the fantastic technology all around us, they wonder why people must continue to go hungry or to live in wretched hovels or to plead for niggardly charity. If there is a service dedicated to the "welfare of mankind" anywhere, shouldn't it be social work? Isn't *it* what service is all about?

CHAPTER 3
THE DEATH OF A PROFESSION?

Indeed, the bottom has fallen out, the lid has blown off, and there is much jostling and pushing among us. Gone are the days when social workers were bright-eyed bearers of glad tidings, wrapped in the enabler's bag and tied with a generic bow.
—Ivor Kraft, addressing social work colleagues at a professional symposium, 1968.

Social work is a profession in crisis. Any crisis—whether in the life of a young adult trying to extricate himself from the protective custody of his parents, or in the life of an entire population attempting to rid itself of an outworn regime—is basically a breakdown of old definitions and old solutions. And as a system casts about for a new definition of itself and its problems, there is a state of flux that is both uncomfortable and bewildering. For most people, then, the term "crisis" has a negative connotation.

But a crisis is also a time of hope: bewilderment is a sign that the system is finally recognizing that the old order is inadequate, and this is always a necessary condition for attaining something better.

The symptoms of crisis in social work are at hand. We have already alluded to some—the loss of credibility with the poor and other alienated elements of society, for example. And then there is that most distressing of storm signals to any profession: the fact that it no longer has a key role, or indeed any role, in some fields to which it previously laid claim.

Federal funds that in the past have helped to shape —nay, often distort—social work education are drying up with alarming rapidity. Social workers have always been identified in the public mind with a "bleeding heart" mentality and with welfare "freeloading." As attitudes toward the poor have hardened in middle-class white America in recent years, social workers have felt the same reaction toward themselves.

Not unlike the dilemma of the minority person who "makes it" in the system, the social worker who flees to the safety of the suburban clinic discovers that to the public he is still the "social worker," still identified with the other America. And like the upwardly mobile minority person, he needs to come to terms with his own identity and his commitment to those values that brought him into social work in the first place.

Paradoxically, at the very time that it is beset by such external adversities, the social work profession is rent by internal conflicts that are unprecedented. These stresses within the profession are important. Not only do they bring into question the ultimate viability of the social work profession, they also tell us much about the dimensions of the crisis and how it may eventually be resolved.

A central issue is the future relationship of social work to its key constituencies—to the poor and disadvantaged who were historically its raison d'être; to the social welfare system that has dominated it; and to the academic institutions in which it has sought professional respectability. As long as social work could hold these respective elements in some sort of uneasy balance, it could maintain the fiction that it and they were in essential harmony. But the last decade has seen the illusion of consensus punctured; the result for social work, as for many other institutions, has been the aforementioned crisis.

This book goes to the heart of the crisis in social work. We believe that the profession cannot continue in its present role of house flunky for welfare institutions, obsessed with professional status in its most superficial sense. Instead, it must carve out a vital role based on its historic commitment to human welfare. It must become a shaper of events instead of remaining something continually shaped by what is happening around it.

We offer the reader two views of the crisis and the road social work must travel. Based on several years of intimate involvement with the profession, each of us has arrived at his own assessment of the state of social work and of the sources of its difficulties, and each offers a solution to its present predicament. One of us sees the problem as being so fundamental that it requires a radical reordering of social work education and even of the concept of "professionalism" itself. The other perceives in recent changes in social work practice and education the beginnings of a renaissance that can create a new professionalism within the framework that is already emerging.

It is perhaps symbolic of the crisis that no single statement seemed adequate to encompass the problem—no single answer seemed adequate to resolve it. Here are the résumés of the two interpretations of the crisis and their implications for the unloved profession.

A SUMMARY OF THE RADICAL CRITIQUE: THERE MUST BE A BASIC REDEFINITION

Social work has been absorbed by a system that permits it to survive on the *system's* terms. The fundamental purpose of the system and that of social work are incongruous. The basic purpose of social work is represented to be the welfare of mankind, while the goal of the system is to maintain itself—to maintain existing structures and power centers. By cooperating with the system, social work helps to maintain the power structure as it is. Therefore, social work's hidden task is to maintain the status quo.

This maintenance of the status quo is most obvious in social work's reluctance to deal straightforwardly with the problems of poverty. Social work has elected *not* to deal with the conditions that cause poverty. Instead, it has isolated certain emotional aberrations as a cause of poverty and has evolved a psychotherapeutic mode for its treatment.

A glance at the catalogs of social work graduate schools provides easy documentation. While psychiatry is no longer the exclusive knowledge-base it once was in social work schools, the emphasis is still strongly on personal and interpersonal dynamics. Fields such as political science and economics, meanwhile, get the merest nods in the programs of the majority of students. It is as if one needed only to know what was "wrong" with the victims of injustice in order to cure the injustice; it is as though being poor is simply an individual aberration and the poor must accept the total guilt for their condition.

But social work has also failed to live up to its contract with the established order. Financed to maintain "things as they are," social work has failed to deliver on its promise. The poor have not remained happy but poor; they have become visible, angry, demanding, and threatening.

Like other institutions, the agencies tend to develop as self-serving, self-perpetuating modules isolating social problems and narrowing potential solutions. Agencies closer to the battlefield, however, have shown more flexibility in their responses than have the schools. While the relationship between schools of social work and service delivery agencies has always been uneasy and competitive, recent developments predict a wider split as the service delivery systems become even more responsive than the traditionally based schools. For example, the Community Service Society of New York—one of the oldest and most established of the social work agencies—has broken with traditional social work practice and is reaching into the community in new directions. The agency says that social work as taught and practiced today no longer meets the needs of people in the community. New efforts are being made by this agency, and there is a discernible erosion of the professional social worker's role in this new service. Another old and "traditional" agency, Catholic Charities, has made a similar move. The dissatisfaction of social service agencies with the professional social worker is growing on every side.

Social work has failed to maintain a position of independence in relation to other "helping" professions. Despite its own strong motivation and overriding concern to assume a "rightful" place among those professions, social work has emerged as their handmaiden—not as a recognized and contributing peer. At interdisciplinary team meetings, social workers are usually the last to be called upon and the least listened to. While this may have something to do with the psychology of the social worker—his acute sense of being a continuously dependent creature—it is also related to a fact that social work has never directly faced: in every area where social workers claim some expertise, there are others who are more expert.

Although the social worker may have a knowledge of psychodynamics, it is the psychiatrist who is the recognized expert. If the social worker claims some expertise in the structure of social institutions, the sociologist is still the expert of record. If expertise is needed in housing and development, the urban planner's knowledge takes precedence. Since social workers labor along very narrow lines of knowledge and action, they are constantly being shunted aside by more confident and acknowledged experts.

Rather than struggle with competing specialists, the social worker needs to opt for the role of expert among experts. By widening rather than narrowing his base of knowledge, he can assume a very appropriate as well as respected role as the *coordinator* of specialized services. When all is said and done, it is the social worker who ultimately delivers the services. He is—or should be—the focal point through which all the other experts' knowledge is funneled.

Rather than specialize his program further, as he is now doing, it would serve him well to *generalize:* to develop in new directions; to become proficient in those areas he has assiduously neglected—economics, anthropology, sociology, etc.; and to improve service delivery. The social worker would gain in acceptance and respectability by becoming the "expert of the experts."

The handmaiden-role social work has assumed for itself is most blatant in its relationship with psychiatry. Social workers remain in a constant state of trembling and awe before this branch of medicine. To be supervised by a psychiatrist is absolutely the last word in their professional development.

Social work literature is replete with the contributions psychiatric thought has made to the field, but little is said about what social work has contributed to psychiatry. In practice it is the psychiatrist who does the "treatment" while it is the social worker who "sees" the family. An unexpected irony is the recent development in psychiatry of an area loosely described as "community psychiatry." Social work has pretty much abandoned the area of community work in its pursuit of a role as psychiatric specialist. The irony lies in the fact that social workers have abandoned the community to become psychiatrists while the psychiatrists are reaching out into the community to become social workers.

As a human being, the social worker is thus caught in a bewildering interplay of forces, counterforces, and ethical dilemmas. On the one hand, there is the strong sense of commitment, of altruism, of humanistic strivings that brought him into the field in the first place. On the other hand there is the exceedingly small bag of skills he is handed from which he is to select his options.

Not unexpectedly, he becomes a creature of conflict and frustration—insecure about his own knowledge, his talents, and his very reason for being—uncertain of what life out there is really all about. He tends to fall back upon a series of protective devices that seem to preserve in him the problems created by his professional role. These devices have practical functions, but the way in which they are used in social work hardly justifies their importance. For the social worker, life is an endless round of conferences and meetings, of continuous supervision, and of threading his way through a system of incredibly intricate agency procedures.

And the process begins when the student of social work undergoes intensive maternalistic observation—his personality is microscopically examined; his brains are picked clean; finally, his compliance is ensured. He is then deemed "professional" enough to be permitted to practice, but his dependency quickly becomes apparent. First there is an agency to determine what he is to do and how he is to do it. Then there is a supervisor with whom he must share his work. He is usually placed in an in-service training program where he has to undo some of what he has learned in school to do. Then there are the reports, recordings, administrative responsibilities, all the make-work projects and justifications for his being there, and all the paper verifications of his professional competence. Even psychiatrists—whom social workers appear so determined to emulate—reach a point at which they get to practice as independent professionals. Not so the social worker. He is inextricably bound to a system of permanent dependency.

The development of social work from a service delivery field into a professional institution has taken place at an enormous price. Social work reveals itself today as a "might-have-been" profession: a profession whose dynamic potential has been channeled into such narrow paths that it makes little impact on today's turbulent social scene—a profession that has so lost its way from its initial purpose of service that it is still struggling for role and identity these many years later.

The movement toward professionalism has been a hallmark of social work since its development into a systematized service delivery field. This has not only meant a shift of emphasis from serving the poor to serving the more hospitable middle class; but there has grown as well an ostrich-like acceptance of the social inequalities in our present system. The recognition of these social inequities produces reflex head-nodding and ritualistic expressions of concern, but that is about all.

The practice of social work in practically all of its dimensions remains essentially middle-class-client-focused. The social worker today is not prepared to understand the current social scene or to assume a meaningful role in it. The "relevancy" of this profession that has attracted so many committed people to its bosom has become even more elusive in the 1970's than it was in the 1940's and 1950's—and even that relevancy may disappear in the 1980's.

Perhaps social work would not have resolved any significant social problems if it had decided to tackle the underlying social system rather than the isolated personality. But it would have been more true to its own rhetoric and code. The significant battles today are being fought *outside* its domain, and the contending forces are beyond its influence.

Social workers must believe that they are able to affect the human condition. They have tended to shy away from fields such as work with the aging and the retarded, clienteles for which there is little or no promise of a glowing future. They gravitate to such fields as child welfare, which is basically future-oriented. By neglecting basic environmental conditions and concentrating on psychic functioning, they have spent most of their energy where it could have the least impact on their clients' lives.

A SUMMARY OF THE CASE FOR REFORM: THE EMERGENCE OF A NEW PROFESSIONALISM

The social work profession was created by social service institutions to serve their manpower needs. These same institutions have continued to dominate social work, whatever the pretensions of social workers about being like the old private entrepreneurial professions such as medicine and law. Service bureaucracies have set the standards of recruitment to social work, controlled the education of social workers, and encased trained workers in a finely developed system of supervision.

For years the institutions of the professional community served the needs of established welfare systems. Insofar as the behavior of social workers was regulated by the professional community at all, it tended to reflect the interests of their employers. When the National Association of Social Workers spoke out on public issues, it called upon spokesmen for the welfare establishment, who essentially repeated what they had said in their official capacity.

In the process, the organized professional community and its educational enterprise subverted the social work mission. The lofty purposes espoused by the profession served as a legitimizing veneer more than a true guide to action. Rather than providing a meaningful alternative to bureaucratic domination, the National Association of Social Workers and the Council on Social Work Education became the instruments of subversion.

Yet, paradoxically, these same professional institutions are the only visible mechanisms capable of mounting a countervailing force sufficient to offset the powerful influence of established social welfare systems. Can they now stop playing handmaiden to these systems, stop reinforcing their values, stop rationalizing social work's participation in the more brutalizing aspects of welfare? What hope is there that the social work profession can now play a different role?

One thing to understand is the *changing* nature of the relationship between the social work profession and the social welfare institutions. Originally there was little to distinguish the two. Not only was social work education molded to reflect the interests of organized social welfare, with professional training little more than a period of apprenticeship. The early professional associations, based on the fields that employed social workers—schools, hospitals, clinics, group-serving agencies—gave their members little sense that they were part of *a* profession, with *a* set of values and expertise.

This was the first stage of professionalization in social work. On the surface it might have appeared that it was the social workers and not the social welfare institutions who were dominating. Although social workers could be found in key positions throughout the social welfare establishment, on closer examination it appears that their outlook was shaped by their organizational and not their professional affiliations. In addition, top decision-making spots tended to be reserved for *non*-professionals.

Perhaps an even more graphic clue to the actual relationship between the social work profession and social welfare institutions is in the fact that the profession could not come near controlling entry to the social work jobs. The vast majority of positions in social welfare continued to be held by persons excluded from the professional ranks, and the general public made no distinction between professional and non-professional personnel.

A second stage of professionalization began with the gradual emergence of a single profession distinct from social welfare institutions, a separate system with its own identity and its own institutional needs. A major milestone in this stage was the establishment in 1955 of the National Association of Social Workers; it replaced the array of separate associations that had existed up to that time. It has progressively developed the tools for professional regulation and united action.

A parallel development occurred in social work education with the Council on Social Work Education. Launched in 1952, it has gained increasing leverage in the affairs of schools of social work. Officially vested with responsibility for accrediting the schools, it has developed real clout only in recent years.

Although this second stage was a necessary stop in the liberation of the social work profession from bureaucratic domination, it has not been a particularly admirable phase. In casting about for a professional identity, social workers tended to follow the model of the entrepreneurial professions. Their emphasis on prolonged education in an academic setting was seized upon by social workers as a means of gaining professional respectability.

The result was that social work failed to distinguish between the real and the superficial aspects of formal education. The master's degree was treated as essential for professionalism, yet the curriculum lacked the intellectual rigor of equivalent programs. And those who gained the master's degree went to jobs that the public viewed as being on a level with schoolteaching (which called for a bachelor's degree at the entry level) and nursing (which in many instances involved non-degree hospital training). Meanwhile, social workers preoccupied with professional status saw private practice and licensing as ways of competing with the images of the established fields.

These pretensions to professional autonomy were largely illusory. Social welfare institutions continued to dominate social work. But this stage had an important function in the process of self-definition. Just as subjugated minority groups need to assert their independence as a means of gaining it, the claim by social workers that they were more than bureaucratic functionaries could help to pave the way for true emancipation from their captive state by setting up a new set of expectations in their minds and in those of their captors.

Social work is now in transition to stage three: the new professionalism. The process is at an extremely critical point because of the powerful pull of the old professionalism and the fragility of the new thrust. It began in the turbulence of urban America in the 1960's. The turbulence and society's initial response to it drove both organized social welfare and the social work profession to experiment with new and more relevant roles—not unlike what happened in the Depression in the

1930's. But just as the ferment of the mid-1930's turned into the reaction and acrimony and witch-hunting of the end of that decade, we have witnessed a souring of the promise in the more recent surge toward change. Organized social welfare, having never really fulfilled the promise of the 1960's, is rapidly turning back to its old ways. The trend is made even more ominous by new technologies of people-control.

Will social work again revert as it has in the past? Admittedly there are enormous pressures for it to do so. To a great extent, the internal struggles in social work are around precisely this issue. The point that many social workers miss is that the ground on which the struggle is being waged is shifting. Social work is not the profession it was in the 1930's. The cleavages within it are more prominent now *because* there is a clearer sense of an organized professional community, capable of making specific and binding demands on its members. Schools of social work are not as free as they were forty years ago to drift with the tide and socialize their students to unquestioning compliance with the norms of the industry; the Council on Social Work Education has committed itself and its member schools to tangible action in behalf of relevance.

When the professional community demands that its members today act as advocates in behalf of social victims—that they put the interests of clients ahead of the interests of their agencies—it cannot suddenly say tomorrow that it didn't really mean it. A new breed of student has been taught to question professors' wisdom and to join in shaping the educational experience. He is not going to be willing to go back to the old style of brainwashing—nor is he going to suddenly stop asking questions when he leaves school and enters practice.

Social work schools and agencies have been engaged in a massive drive to recruit minority-group members. And as they enter in substantial numbers, these new elements in the field view their role in political as well as technical terms. They are making demands—not only in their own behalf but in behalf of their brethren still struggling in the urban mire. They will not suddenly become docile. Thus, even were social work's leadership ready to duck and run in the face of repression and reaction, the new brand of social worker would not allow it to do so.

By and large, social work still does serve the interests of the welfare industry above all others. Social work education has yet to sort out intellectual substance from intellectual froth. And it still has to develop the tools that can convert high aspirations into effective action. But out of the urban crisis has come a vision of what social work can become, of the new professionalism. Will social work complete the transition? Social work owes it to the countless people—the victims of a harsh social order—whom it has failed in the past. It also owes it to the earnest social workers who have devoted their lives to this unloved profession.

SECTION 2
THE RADICAL CRITIQUE: THERE MUST BE A BASIC REDEFINITION

The social problems facing contemporary society have erupted much too quickly for a cautious, pedantic profession to deal with them. Being alive in the 1950's has scarcely prepared anyone for life in the 1970's. The social turbulence, above all the demands of the poor and the disenfranchised, in fact, the whole thrust of the profound counter-Establishment movement that was spawned in the last few years have presented baffling problems for the here and now. They are staggering to face and bewildering to all of us—but these are precisely the problems social work *must* face up to if it is to have any meaning at all. These problems can no longer be ignored, reduced to sophistry, or left for nameless others to contend with. This is the task and the monumental challenge of social work today.

The history of social work militates against a meaningful reform. Its periodic revisions have thus far served only to reinforce its drift, enmeshing it that much more in the machinery of the Establishment.

Reforms can easily be the subject of in-house professional chitchat, but can reforms really do the job? The introduction of a new course in school, the public embrace of a "relevancy" or "advocacy" concept, the removal of a tie by a social worker here, an academic discussion of the "black-white issue" or the "chicano problem" there—what do they really accomplish? One thing they do accomplish is to alienate further those populations social work purports to be reaching, by substituting rhetoric for action and promises for delivery. These seasonal reforms also serve to alienate those who really can make social work deliver on what social work has been promising for so long—those who are idealistic and non-cynical—those who are concerned and committed—those who take words at

their face value and actually try to translate them into practice.

In many systems reforms are gratuitous and are instituted to ensure a continuance of power rather than to implement real change. This writer is suggesting that even the best-intentioned reforms will only serve to continue social work as a handmaiden profession—a might-have-been profession—and will guarantee its continuance as the unloved profession.

A much bolder approach than mere reform is needed for these times: for example, taking social work out of the universities and putting it back into the community where it belongs.

The search for professionalism, the very concept of professionalism, in social work is bankrupt. It has failed to deliver in the past and offers no promise for delivery in the future.

What has happened to social work has not been the result of any evil intent. Social workers are at heart good, humanitarian, well-intentioned, altruistic people intensely dedicated to the public weal. They cannot be faulted for seeking rewards and recognition for their efforts—this is the goal of all within our society. This striving for recognition, however, has had an important part to play in the current agony of social work. What has really befallen social work, what has really brought it to its present-day staggering, ineffective state, has been the rigid institutionalization of its practice within the labyrinthine social welfare industry and the ossification of its training program. Social work training—the educational ritual that gives the social worker his credentials and which maintains the tenor, philosophy, values, and attitudes that infuse social work practice—must be looked at in some depth. If there is a villain in the history of social work it is probably the educational mills that grind out the human material to feed the social welfare industry.

A "radical" position sees the schools of social work as being primarily responsible for the crisis in the profession today. But it must be remembered that the schools themselves are mandated by the social welfare industry to train and certify the professional worker. The field is as much responsible for what social workers are as the training institutions themselves.

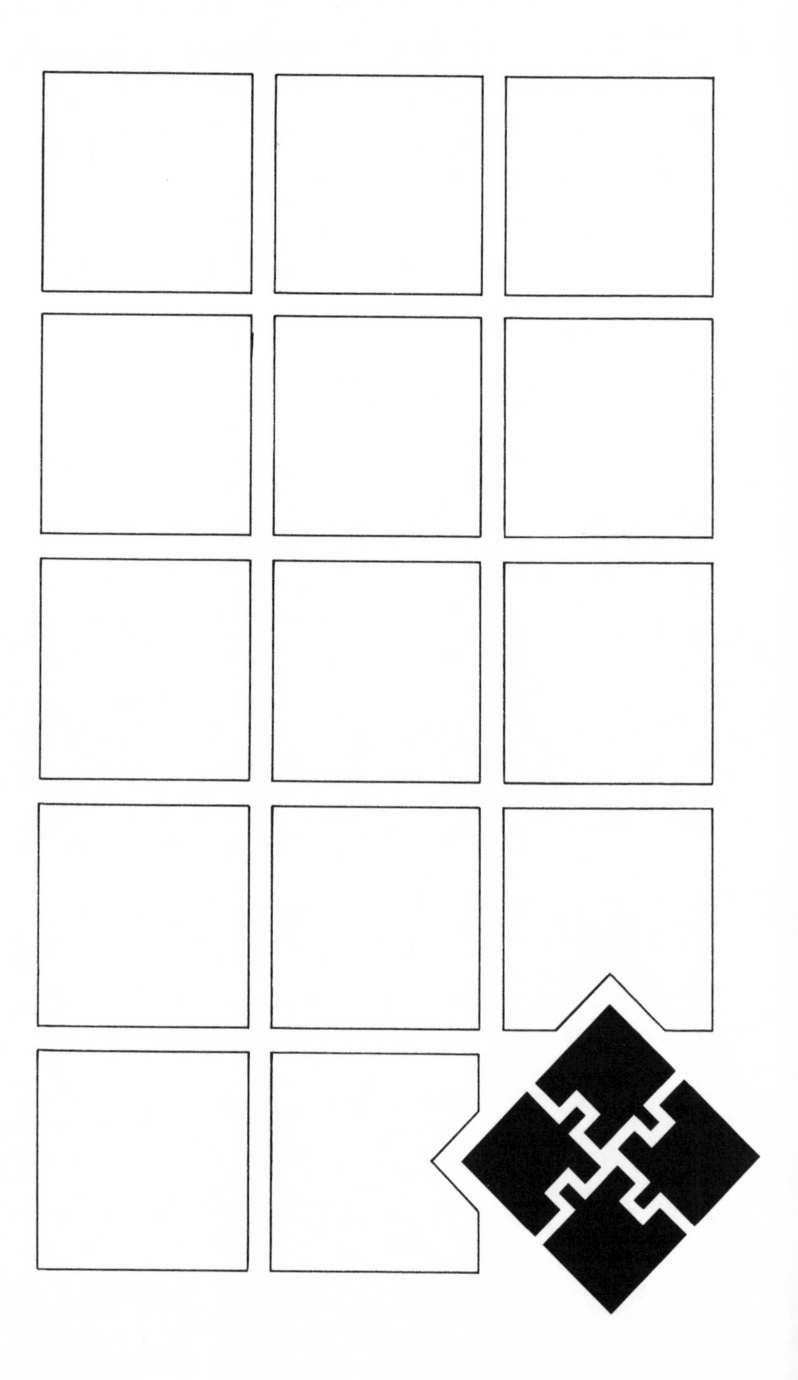

CHAPTER 4
TRAINING FOR DEPENDENCY—THE EDUCATION OF THE SOCIAL WORKER

It takes six years of academic training—four years of undergraduate and two years of graduate school—to produce a professional social worker who is prepared for a career of supervision in a service institution. Even then the product is considered less than finished.

At one time the master's degree in social work (M.S.W.) was recognized as *the* terminal degree for practice.* With the growth of social work into areas of specialization and its concomitant bureaucratic development, areas are now being carved out where the master's degree no longer serves as a passport for practice. Most noticeably, this has occurred in social work education, where the doctorate is now a necessary certificate for the teaching of social work fledglings. Needless to say, the doctorate is the symbol of academic attainment rather than practice skill.

As any practitioner recognizes, scholastic achievement is not necessarily congruent with practice skills. Perhaps the contrary—for the time and energy required for the degree pursuit must be taken from practice. Hence, we are presented with a situation in which the teachers of graduate social work—a practice field if there ever was one—may have the least practice experience or skills. Although there are current grumblings, no efforts have been formalized to require teachers of social work to maintain time in practice to continue eligibility for teaching. Some do on their own, but not too many. A separation between teaching and practice occurs, and every day the separation grows.

---

* In recent years the bachelor's degree in social work is being promoted as the "credential" for social work practice—at least in those bodies that authorize these credentials, the Council on Social Work Education and the National Association of Social Workers. In reality, however, the master's degree in social work continues to be acknowledged as *the* degree establishing professional credentials by most of the agencies in the social welfare industry.

While most other master's programs lead to degrees after one year (thirty credits) of graduate training, social work degrees are awarded after two years (sixty credits). This extended time span may be seen as indicating the difficulties in attaining practice skills. It may also be related to the insecurity social work has about itself, its problems of identification, and its perception of itself in the hierarchical ranks of other professional practice fields. Movements are gaining ground to reduce graduate training from a two-year to a one-year program, with the fourth year of undergraduate college as the first year of specialization in social work.

From 1952 to 1970 there was an ever-increasing number of students enrolled in master's programs of graduate schools of social work, the number almost quadrupling, from 3,944 in 1952 to 12,821 in 1970.[1] Degrees awarded during that time period ranged from 1,946 in the 1951–52 period to 5,638 in the 1969–70 academic year. During the two decades from 1951 through 1970, approximately 52,000 social workers passed through schools of social work and were certified for entering practice in the United States.

Training for any specialty involves an exclusion factor. Not everyone can be a brain surgeon, nor can everyone be a social worker. It may be of interest to assess briefly who does and who does not go into the graduate schools of social work.

Because of social work's historic concern for minorities, as well as current popular movements in civil rights, schools of social work have become more sensitive to the racial distribution of their student bodies. As Table 3 shows, in 1970 76 percent of the student bodies at graduate schools of social work were white, approximately 14 percent were black, with the remaining 10 percent drawn from other minority groups. According

Table 3
Ethnic Characteristics of Full-Time Degree Students Enrolled in Graduate Schools of Social Work—1970

	First Year	Percent	Second Year	Percent
White	5,699	75.0	4,757	77.0
Black	975	14.5	872	14.3
Chicano	120	1.8	108	1.7
American Indian	16	0.6	11	0.1
Asian-American	99	1.5	52	0.9
Other United States	119	1.8	102	1.7
Other foreign	118	1.8	109	1.7
Total	7,146	97.0	6,011	97.4

Source: *Statistics in Social Work* Education (New York: Council on Social Work Education, 1970).

to current census figures, blacks represent approximately 12 percent of the current population. This may seem to indicate that blacks proportionally represent their population percentage in schools of social work. However, thought must be given to the purposes of social work as well as to the population it is attempting to serve—the poor, generally consisting of minorities. Schools of social work are sensitive to the lack of minority representation, both in their student bodies and on their faculties, and they have engaged in outreach recruitment. This has met with some success. Table 4 indicates that there has been appreciable change in racial distribution of social work students from 1953 to 1970.

Despite the efforts made by schools of social work to

Table 4
Racial Distribution of Social Work Students, from 1953 to 1970

Race	Academic Year 1953–1954	Academic Year 1960–1961	Academic Year 1969–1970
White	87%	86%	76%
Non-white	13%	14%	24%

Source: *Statistics in Social Work Education* (New York: Council on Social Work Education, 1970).

enlist more minority members in their ranks and their degree of success in doing so, racial representation of minority groups still remains a real problem for the schools.

Linked with minority representation and operating as an important exclusion factor have been the skyrocketing costs of social work education. Social work schooling is a fulltime program. In addition to academic learning (classes, research, papers, etc.), three-fifths of the student's time is spent in intensive field training. The program is sufficiently demanding to permit the student little opportunity for the pursuit of academic areas of interest, much less any paid employment, during this time. Many graduate students with family responsibilities would be hard-pressed to engage in this academic endeavor unless they were receiving considerable supplementation, such as an agency or school scholarship. For a married man this would mean the wife's employment. Unless one is really affluent, even a working spouse may not be enough to make the cost affordable. Scholarships and free-tuition grants have been the survival factor for many students, but these were much more available during the 1950's and 1960's. The 1970's are marked by the increasing costs of education and the drying up of available funds for educational purposes.

The fact that the cost of social work education is making it less accessible to the poor is reflected in statistics on family income of entering students. In 1966, the last year for which the Council on Social Work Education has figures, 18 percent of first-year students came from families with incomes under $5,000. Six years earlier it had been 32 percent. Meanwhile, the percentage from families with incomes over $20,000 nearly doubled.[2]

The economics of graduate education also have impact on the sexual distribution of social work students. Historically a field established by women, social work continues to be a field where women outnumber the men.

Table 5

Students Enrolled in Graduate Schools of Social Work, by Sex and Class—November, 1970

Sex	First Year	Second Year	Total
Male	2,605	2,395	5,000
Female	4,211	3,992	8,203

Source: *Statistics in Social Work Education* (New York: Council on Social Work Education, 1970).

Interestingly enough, in third- and fourth-year graduate programs, men predominate:

Table 6
Students Enrolled in Graduate Schools of Social Work, by Sex and Class—November, 1970

Sex	Third Year	Fourth Year	Total
Male	146	138	284
Female	76	43	119

Source: *Statistics in Social Work Education* (New York: Council on Social Work Education, 1970).

From 1931 to 1960 there was a rise in the male student population from 1,270 to 4,070. In 1970 the percentage of male students dropped slightly to 38 percent. The women continue to dominate in schools of social work on the graduate level, while the men come into their own in the post-master's programs.

Admission to graduate schools of social work is predicated on a number of factors: undergraduate grades, letters of reference, a written statement with some emphasis on autobiographical information, and stated reasons for entering the field. This is followed by an admissions interview.

The admissions interview is in essence a probe of the candidate's life, history, attitudes, educability, and motivation for his pursuit of social work study. As many students can attest, the admissions interview, with its demands for the sharing of experiences and feelings that one would only share in a psychiatric interview (and even then only after a period of time spent in the establishment of trust), can be a brutally searching procedure. It can be either a perfunctory or meaningful experience, depending upon the skills of the interviewer and the orthodoxy of the school applied to.

While it may be claimed that this process ensures the continuation of a professional elite of a particular personality-cast in social work education and practice, it does serve to screen out people with obvious personality characteristics that may be potentially destructive to others or themselves.

Admissions are primarily guided by one's suitability for functioning as a potential psychotherapist rather than a social worker. Few, if any, questions, for example, are asked about attitudes toward economic systems, toward sociological theories, about political attitudes, or about activism in the contemporary scene. When these do happen to come up in interview, they are defined in terms of personality or character, these being deemed the sole criteria for eventual performance as a social worker. Social workers as a group have a particularly insidious way of casting all events into analytic analogues. To be overly critical of a particular system would be a "conflict with authority" or an "unresolved Oedipal." If overdone, these kinds of assessments can mean a rank denial of reality, which can become an automatic protective device—particularly for the one doing the "interpretation." Social workers, unfortunately, are particularly vulnerable in this area. The admission process continues the control of entering students in accordance with the existing biases of the field. Admissions interviews are felt to be costly and in some instances unreliable predictors of candidates' potential and are being phased out in many schools. Reliance then falls more heavily upon written material—the autobiographical statement, the experience of the student, his references, and his previous academic record.

Despite the fact that social work is in essence a field of *doing,* scholastic achievement looms large in the determination of the candidate's suitability for admission. As part of a university system, a graduate program in social work uses the same scholastic criteria for admission as are used for admission to a graduate program in English or mathematics or engineering. Moreover, continuation in school is subject to the same academic rules that govern other graduate schools in the university.

What this has meant for social work, however, has been an exclusion of students who may be admirably suited for social work, having the necessary qualities of empathy, interest and concern for people, etc., but who, for various reasons, lack the academic credentials. This has resulted in the unplanned but very real exclusion of a rich and potentially revitalizing force from the field.

Since the school issues the passport to practice, the social worker in training comes to recognize its power very early in the game. The name of the game is respect for the power and control that the schools exercise. There is really no possibility of professional practice without the M.S.W., and the schools zealously guard their prerogatives for credential issuance.

Graduate training for the social worker is divided into two sections: the class and the field. Although there is variation in the practice of the seventy currently accredited schools of social work in the United States, most students spend two days per week in school and three days a week in the field.

The field is the arena of practice—usually an agency where the student deals with a selected number of working assignments under the close supervision of an experienced field instructor. Field placements are selected by the school and must meet standards of practice acceptable by the school. There is considerable variation as to what those standards are, and frequently these standards are unrealistic. What is deemed acceptable reflects the biases of the schools. The newer and more innovative agencies, of course, are rejected by the more traditional schools. (An interesting aside is that some schools will not approach an agency themselves to request student placements, but will wait for the agency to apply to them. This is another indication of the prestige-conscious game that is such a damnable irritant in this allegedly humanistic field.) Many agencies are simply so repelled by the paper work, the forms, the bureaucratic details, and the meaningless statistics that the school requires that they simply wash their hands of having students at all. One agency administrator said that upon his application for students he received from the school a packet of materials so thick that it would have required a week of his time to wade through it. He returned the packet (at considerable postage) and remained studentless.

It is tacitly admitted but rarely acknowledged that the field represents the most valid of the educational experiences a student may receive during his two years of graduate training.

The field is, in effect, an industry committed to providing a variety of services for its clients. The school has a prime educational responsibility for providing the social worker with tools of practice. Having students in an agency represents—from the agency's point of view—a surrendering of space and resources to students who will render limited service to their client population. An agency worker may, for example, have a caseload of thirty or more, while the student over the course of an academic year may service from eight to ten clients. One wonders what the agency gets from this allocation of space and time for students.

The agency has a justifiable stake in the education of social workers. Agencies have hopes of recruiting staff from the students; they offer scholarships to students with future commitments of time and service in payment. Agencies with mediocre professional service ratings can bolster their prestige by having students present. Other agencies see and sometimes exploit students to bolster their own thin ranks of personnel. One student entered an agency to find twelve cases heaped on her desk demanding services—on her first day as a student!

The relationship between social work education and social work practice can be strained. While the schools continue to believe that they are establishing the criteria and terms of practice, the field agencies have their own position. They patiently lie in wait while the student goes through the formal ministrations of the educational rites, and then, seizing upon the fledgling graduate, proceed to educate him in terms of practice realities—perhaps "re-educate" would be a better word.

Adequate field placements can be difficult, particularly with the decreasing availability of funds for social services. In the New York area, for example, six schools of social work compete for available space, and student field assignments must be within the limits of geographical possibility. Schools have been attempting to establish more student units with school faculty as teachers. This seems to offer a more enhancing learning experience for the students. For one thing, it permits the employment of group-teaching techniques and the privilege of sharing with one's fellows in the learning experience.

The relationship between agencies with students and schools has been a difficult one. The school is ever-zealous in the protection of the student during his two-year stay. The student identifies more with the agency since this is where his clients are, and the relationship between client and student, by nature of the student's investment in time and effort, is quite strong. The agency generally is strongly criticized by the student for many of its practices, but the client remains supreme.

In order to ensure "adequate education" for the student—in effect to maintain its control over his heart and mind—the school engages in a series of procedures to maintain the primary identification of the student with the school. The school mounts a force of classroom teachers called field advisers or faculty advisers, who assume responsibility for the student's field education. These advisers visit the students in the agency, read their material, and confer with the field teacher regarding the learning problems of the students and the teaching problems of the field teacher. Courses in "field teaching" are offered by the school to the instructors in the field to keep them abreast of the latest academic thought and practice.

Grading remains a school function. While the field instructor produces an evaluation of the student's performance, the faculty adviser's evaluation of the student—which contains both his evaluation of field performance and of classroom performance—is the crucial document in the student's academic life.

This complex alliance between school and field is maintained by a network of tentacles that the school has spread to the field: faculty advisers, faculty field teachers, and a series of ritualistic meetings held between the field and the school. Since the ends are different—academic achievement on the one hand and service delivery on the other—this alliance appears doomed. Just as social work's hopes tend to clash with the status quo-ism of the Establishment, the ends and aims of field and school also conflict.

Within the school itself, advocates of areas of concentration—group work, casework, and community organization—contend for bureaucratic power. Within the concentrations themselves, respective ideologies are also in constant contention. The students entering the schools of social work are faced with a bewildering array of systems that are not always functioning in orchestral harmony. The students are also faced with a bewildering array of people with whom they must relate.

Social work education, unlike other academic disciplines, is not predicated on intellectual prowess alone. Naïve students quickly come to realize that survival is highly dependent upon one's ability to manipulate the academic system. Some take refuge in a type of passive invisibility, contributing just enough for recognition but not enough to create waves or firm identification. Others rapidly learn what attitudes are permissible and become vociferous advocates. Some identify closely with members of various ideologies to ensure survival. Even breaking rules is acceptable providing sufficient anger is expressed. A pseudo-militancy is encouraged. All students come quickly to recognize the rules of gamesmanship and make corresponding adjustments to them. Most students come away with the feeling that a large percentage of academic work in school is necessary nonsense—nonsense because of its lack of content and necessary because it leads to the M.S.W., the passport to social work practice. What students do come to realize is that one must be most respectful of the "passport office" or he simply does not "travel."

Perhaps apocryphal, but unfortunately possible, is the following story: During the student rebellions at Columbia in the late 1960's, the social work students —the "defenders of the underdog"—were notably absent from the action. "And where were you when we needed you?" asked the leaders of the rebellion. The social workers' response was painfully real. "Our survival in school," they contended, "is based not only on our ability to do the required intellectual work, but also upon our attitudes, behavior, and our activities. Participation can easily spell the end of our professional careers!"

This story brings up an unfortunate point: overall the message to the students is obedience—obedience to the form and the content of a particular academic system. One must attend class, do one's papers, do one's research, take one's tests, and "relate"—with all its invidious as well as positive connotations. While perhaps appropriate for other academic disciplines, for the social worker this dependency, this obedience to a system, has a profound effect upon his working career —the system itself becomes a giver. It is not to be challenged, it is not to be fought—it is to be taken as is. It is what is casually referred to as the "reality." And who in their right minds will fight "reality"? Very practically it means for the social worker that it is necessary to adapt to the reality of the agency—to accept the condition that his supervision will be interminable—to accept the reality that this is agency practice and either take it or leave it.

In a larger sense the social worker is trained to accept the reality of the social conditions around him (conditions he never really learned about anyway). A social injustice fighter? Where? How? An advocacy spokesman for his client? By what right does he aspire to this? How was he prepared, how trained? The social worker is a more dependent creature than an angry client. Professionals don't get angry; professionals don't picket or march in the streets. And, of course, this is the message transmitted to his client—conform, accept, and obey the rules. What becomes of the principle of self-determination when the social worker himself has so narrowly defined his own area of choice? What is it that he preaches that he himself cannot practice?

A unique factor in social work education is the role of the faculty adviser. In schools of social work the faculty adviser assumes dimensions of importance as yet unknown in any other graduate school. He is *the* person in the student's life. He is responsible for the student's classroom performance, field performance, scholarship application, course selection, and overall decision-making as to whether or not the student is permitted to be finally certified as a professional social worker or "counseled out" of the program. Tremendous investments of faculty energy and time are directed into discharging the responsibilities of this office: required contacts with other student instructors, periodic visits to student field placements, reading of student field work material, conferences with field work instructors, meeting with students, assisting in placement planning, and preparation of student references. While most faculty combine advising with teaching duties, faculty are also hired exclusively for faculty advisory roles.

The role of the faculty adviser in graduate schools of social work has grown to overwhelming proportions. While the adviser is still subject to controls by various committees (students have won representation on various committees that decide whether or not students are to remain in programs, etc.) and by school administration, he still has considerable voice in the student's life. The faculty adviser role is one of the most difficult to interpret to universities in dealing for budget allocations, since it has become a rather unique development of schools of social work.

The development of the faculty adviser's function typifies the overweening, maternalistic attitude social work schools have assumed over the lives of their students. With maternalism comes infantilization, and unlike any other graduate student, the social work student rapidly comes to realize that he may not be the mature adult he thought he was after spending four years in undergraduate education. Many of the courses offered are required, and very few electives are available.

Above and beyond the academic requirements, however, the student is exposed to a much more subtle and much more demanding expectation. This is the demand for "participation." Participation in social work school goes beyond sharing of knowledge or questions of intellectual interest. Participation also requires the sharing of attitudes, beliefs, and particularly the sharing of "feelings." The sharing of feelings, or what often really passes for feelings, has become an end in itself, regardless of the particular content of the courses. Self-awareness—a key concept in social work education—has a particularly significant importance in the field: an awareness of one's feelings is necessary in the service delivery system. The student ofttimes feels that he is being "psyched out"; that is, that the demands for feeling-exposure go beyond the area of importance for work or course requirements and are intrusive upon him as a human being. The demand for feeling-exposure is all-pervasive—in his work with clients in the field and in many of the courses he takes in school. Many students seek out psychotherapy, others play the system's game, exposing enough to meet the demands but not enough to be personally bruised in the process.

Concomitant with the demand for exposure of one's feelings is the demand to learn to "relate" and "communicate" with one's fellows and teachers in the field.

Social work has developed a particular pretentiousness in its communications systems. Its use of language is noted for both its extensive and euphemistic quality. Social-workese contains lists of synonyms for "poor"; it contains liberal doses of arcane psychoanalytic jargon; its sentence structure is beyond belief. It tends to belabor the obvious, piling up paragraphs of awesome prose communicating as little as possible. It has borrowed some aspects of the literature of sociology, a field that seems to specialize in non-communication. It has been not so jokingly suggested that social work might be better taught in the Berlitz schools.

Method courses, courses that teach the student how to practice in the field, are mandatory in the schools. Method—be it casework, group work, or community organization—is selected by the student, usually upon entrance (during his state of presumed naïveté), and it remains his principal area of concentration. In the four semesters of the graduate student's life, a method course is usually required in each semester. Method courses parallel field work study, and this is the area most criticized by students. Complaints concern the redundancy of the courses and their meaninglessness, and their use of "canned" vs. live material from the field.

"Canned material" often reflects work with middle-class clients who are intelligent, verbal, and affluent, and who have middle-class aspirations. Beginning students often become impatient with these courses, since their initial enthusiasm and concern for getting on with the basic business of social work has not yet been systematized out. All too often the content is mediocre, not sufficiently intellectually challenging—the biggest complaints about maternalism result from these courses—and is replete with "busy work," paper-writing, and research with no particular focus but to give academic creditability for the offering of the course. A good practical field experience often pales the method courses into obscurity.

Since social work to a large extent has failed to meet its primary charge and responsibility, it is interesting to note its opting for specialist roles. This must be viewed as part of its continual struggle for recognition as a technical skill. The difficulty with this is that it results in the further fragmentation of man functioning in environmental relationships. Reaching fewer and fewer people with greater "expertise," it continues to foster the illusion of the difference between men rather than their basic common denominator.

What has worked for the natural sciences—the breakdown of the universe into smaller and smaller fragments for study—does not necessarily work for the social sciences, even less for social work with its broad and comprehensive perspectives. Glancing at the catalog of a prestigious school of social work, one senses the continuing fractionalization and particularization of services. In the casework area, the following courses are offered in addition to the mandatory methods courses: casework with children; casework relative to psychotic and borderline clients; casework treatment of problems in marriage adjustment; casework with acting-out clients; and family treatment in casework.

The trend is similar to the current movement in medicine: the vanishing family doctor. Who deals now with the whole person or family in the whole human environment? The magnifying lens is reversed. Rather than viewing man in increasingly smaller fragments, he should be viewed in increasingly larger perspectives.

The political facts of academic life have diverted large amounts of energy from the teaching of practice skills. Academia is historically identified with scholarship and the niche of a practice component is at best uncomfortable. It is perhaps more important for one to discuss, research, document, codify, justify, than to engage in the actual doing itself. In identifying the university system as being the determinant of acceptability for practice, social work has traded prestige and respectability for a trousseau of encumbrances that serve to strangle rather than to liberate.

The emasculation of the practice component in social work—social work is relatively meaningless without its practice—is easily illustrated by Table 7.

Table 7
Number of Full-Time Faculty in Graduate Schools of Social Work, by Class, Field Instruction, and Administration, and by Academic Rank, November 1, 1970

	Class Faculty	Field Faculty	Administration
Full Professor	303	8	105
Associate Professor	471	83	53
Assistant Professor	424	377	49
Instructor	95	205	40

Source: *Statistics in Social Work Education* (New York: Council on Social Work Education, 1970).

Field teachers dominate in the lower ranks—instructor and assistant professor—and they become increasingly less visible as one moves up the academic hierarchy. The farther one is removed from the practice component, so the message reads, the more likely he is to attain academic rewards. The criterion for the attainment of academic rank is scholarship—not practice. This point must be emphasized: social work's justification for being lies in its practice. Its scholarly attainments are usually overshadowed by the experts in other fields of the behavioral sciences.

While field teaching occupies the bulk of the student's life, it receives, of course, the least recognition for its services. The less time spent in work with clients, the greater the possibility of rewards.

The attainment of academic rank brings with it not only the attainment of prestige and monetary rewards, but also a deciding voice in the educational character of the school. The training of social workers continues to lie in the hands of those farthest away from the arenas of action.

As the schools move toward academic recognition they are farther removed from the existing ramparts of practice: the agency. Always implicit in the agency attitude toward the schools has been a "let-them-certify-them-and-then-we-will-educate-them" notion. While agencies have their own problems with boards and bureaucratic institutionalization, their mandate for the provision of service remains constant. As the schools pursue their own ends in academia, so do the agencies in practice. Their goals, despite their rhetoric, are becoming increasingly divergent.

A case in point was the recent action of the Community Service Society of New York and the reaction to this in some academic circles. Founded in 1848, "the Community Service Society [CSS] is the largest voluntarily supported, non-profit, non-sectarian family agency in the nation." [3] Until 1970, CSS functioned as a model of "traditional" casework services, offering direct help to individuals and troubled families. It was a model placement agency for casework students because of its attention to individual and family needs and its psychiatric emphasis. CSS "had pioneered in the development and refinement of social work education and practice in the United States." [4] Its staff of approximately 450 consisted largely of social workers and para-professionals; its services generally were restricted to individuals and family service.

A dramatic shift occurred in 1970. In a study made in that year assessing the problems besetting New York City, "[CSS] . . . could do no less than question the very basis of the agency's existence—its relevance to the great needs in these quickly changing times . . . to find new ways to be relevant for the vast number of people who desperately need help in this fast-deteriorating city." [5] CSS announced a major policy shift "in the agency's methods of helping individuals and improving the conditions in the community which affect the welfare of these individuals." [6] CSS decided to place services in the various communities, with neighborhood organizations and local citizens running and operating these services. They had concluded that traditional professional ways of reaching people were ineffective—"helping individuals cannot really get at the heart of the matter"—and they began to devote their services to meeting the "complex of social ills that bears on the individual, not just on the individual himself." [7]

The policy shift of CSS created considerable controversy in academic circles. One of the New York schools of social work forwarded a letter signed by students and faculty indicating their concern about the attempted change in direction from a caseworkbased service to a community systems orientation. It requested them to take a more "pioneer position as an agency in redefining family casework as a neighborhood service." CSS replied, ". . . It was our considered judgment that times have changed, needs have changed, and the methods used in meeting the needs have changed if we as trustees are to discharge our responsibility to make the very best utilization of the funds available to us for the solution of the pressing problems facing the citizens of New York." [8]

It is significant to note the degree of resistance with which CSS's proposed changes in approach were met. Aside from the school calling the CSS method "buckshot," there was no detailed critique of the proposal CSS was offering.

This incident, important in the overall academic stance of social work, typifies the tendency toward rigidity and resistance to change inherent in academic structures. This is not to say that the CSS move was universally disapproved by the schools—certainly it had its champions—but the schools themselves, perhaps by the very nature of their being schools, represent less an innovative force and more a force committed to preserving established practice and procedures. The closer one is to the practice of social work, the more one realizes that certain principles and concepts are no longer viable. It is not necessarily true that removal from the action would lend greater objectivity to perspective—far from it. As far as social work goes, academia has meant for the field an absorption into another system—a system of scholarship whose ends lead in directions other than those of practice.

A dispute sometimes surfaces as to where the innovations and new directions in social work originate—with both the academic and the practice areas laying claim to the achievement. The test of one's tools is in their ability to accomplish results, and often the stress of crisis under which social workers generally operate demands innovations that may be later formalized by academia.

Current treatment modalities being taught in schools are: advocacy, the social worker representing the client; crisis intervention, limited intervention in the client's life at a point of crisis to assist him to return to his condition prior to the crisis; conjoint therapy, the social worker interacting with multiple clients in a given situation; and others. These modalities appear to have arisen in response to the actual work with people. They have been formalized by the schools; that is, identified as specific techniques. Through the formalization process these modalities have become identified as compartmentalized and not considered as part of a social worker's overall response to clients' situations. There is very little stress on the overriding similarities of all these treatment modalities. Thus a social worker can become an expert in conjoint therapy and know nothing about crisis intervention.

The position that social work does not have an intellectual component is an untenable one. Whether this intellectual component is its "unique body of knowledge" as taught in schools of social work is another story. For the most part this body of knowledge is a popularization of Freudian principles. The uniqueness of social work lies in its being the receptacle for all knowledge of man incorporated into a practice tool. Social work's area of expertise is simply its eclectic viewpoint. It is a borrowing field, and the more it borrows and puts into practice the more vital it becomes. It has, however, opted for specialization.

There is no area in which a social worker is "expert" in which other professionals are not *more* "expert." In human relationships psychiatrists are better trained and in therapy they are the acknowledged experts; in the study of social systems sociology claims expertise; for studying the cities' problems there is the urban planner; and on it goes through every area in which social workers claim expertise. The social workers' expertise lies, in fact, in their non-expertise—in their ability to translate all available expertise into the meeting of human needs.

A science fiction story [9] describes a spaceship run by creatures from various parts of the galaxy. Each creature has developed an area of expertise to an incredible degree. Thus one creature was "the Eye," another "the Engine," another "the Talker," another "the Feeder," and so on. Putting all this intensely sophisticated machinery in one space would seem to ensure a fantastically efficient spaceship. However, the ship could not move without the "pusher"—the coordinator of all the expert services. Without overextending the analogy, the coordinator-image is an excellent concept for the social worker: the coordinator of all knowledges plugged into the business of meeting mankind's needs. The "push" of the social work schools has not been toward the coordinator role. The push is toward specialization; a narrow focus on treatment modalities.

Other problems involved in social work education plague all educational institutions: rising costs, physical location, the question of grading, the multiplication of administrative offices. Ivan Illich in *Deschooling Society* [10] raises serious questions as to the efficacy of educational institutions as presently structured. Not only does he posit that being "schooled" has conditioned us to accept institutionalized services as a substitute for what real learning is all about, he also documents the rising costs of institutional education and he refers consistently to the fact that most people acquire most of their knowledge outside of school. Schools, he claims, "are designed on the assumption that there is a secret to everything in life, that the quality of life depends on knowing that secret, that secrets can be known only in orderly succession, and that only teachers can properly reveal these secrets."

The myth of secrets possessed only by the educators is exemplified in schools of social work. Early in the game many students come to recognize that only in the field, or in practice, will real learning occur.

Schools, being the repositories of knowledge, serve as agents of exclusivity rather than inclusivity. Entrance into a school of social work is marked by a system of preordained rites, certifications, and successful passage through institutionalized processes. Students applying to schools of social work do not represent masses of underprivileged or minority groups seeking betterment of living for their people; they primarily consist of social conformists with ideological qualms —mostly middle-class whites seeking resolution for social guilt or seeking a comfortable profession with humanistic overtones.

Who "knows" the poor better than the poor? Who can be closer to the realities of being dispossessed than the dispossessed? In problems of drug addiction and alcoholism, whatever little success has been achieved has resulted from addicts and alcoholics helping each other; e.g., Synanon, A.A., and Phoenix House. Treatment of mental disorders has been often successful in cases where the treating person either has latent problems in the area he has treated or has successfully come to terms with these problems.

By the time the minority member or the poor representative reaches eligibility for entrance into the schools of social work, he has been thoroughly institutionalized and brainwashed, and has "achieved" in Establishment terms. Only at that point is entrance considered into the magic halls of professional service. Social work education simply is not available to the dispossessed, and yet social work has so much to learn from them. It has been their own strident challenges that have led to any possibilities of changing their conditions, but the causes and the amelioration of these conditions are what social work is supposed to be all about.

The issue of racism being voiced in schools of social work in regard to both faculty and students is essentially a cover-up for a much more basic and prevalent fault: namely, professional exclusion. The exclusion of the dispossessed or the uninstitutionally educated from this profession is practiced *without* discrimination; it is totally democratic in nature. Professionalism has its rewards: money, power, prestige—the fewer available to share this pie, the more available for the professionals. A cartoon in the *Saturday Review* showed members of a gang divvying up the loot. A crowd is hovering around the table when the leader announces: "The share of the proceeds of our last bank job comes to $12.95 each—we gotta break up the gang."

If the exclusion of student social workers were directly related to color—keep the blacks out—the issue of racism would have more validity. But *all* the poor are being kept out.

The nature of social work education today is to deny or to discriminate against those who cannot deal effectively with theoretical formulations. Since these formulas are couched in neo-Freudian conceptual terms or in neo-sociological concepts—based on academic in-house rhetoric—they are obviously beyond the grasp of the poor, who are considered non-academic, non-abstract in thinking, and concrete in terms of their needs and wants.

To sum up: there is an extensive range of problems besetting social work in its alliance with the university system–an alliance that serves neither partner adequately and that is largely responsible for the emasculated state in which social work has found itself to be in the 1970's.

There is an increasing institutionalization of the field that has come about as a result of this union: social work's further slippage into the machinery of the Establishment.

There is a difficulty in negotiating the academic system—no small matter when we consider the bureaucratic functioning of that system, the case nature of its operations, and its endemic political struggles.

There is an increasing separation of the knowledge-base of social work from the field of practice. As more and more schoolteachers of social work have progressively less experience in practice, the educational content becomes proportionately less related to the world of social injustice and inhumanity. The uneasy alliance social work has made with the university has necessarily resulted in the upgrading of scholarly pursuits and the downgrading of the practice component. Evidence of this has already been cited in the weakened position field instruction has in curriculum. Trends are now moving toward the elimination of the practice component altogether; the drive toward increased specialization and postgraduate credentials will ensure that.

There is a tendency to narrow the definition of social work still further to maintain its position in the mainstream of psychotherapeutic thought—and also the extensive and scholarly research that has been done in that area—guaranteeing social work's respectability in the university.

There is a continual upwardly mobile movement toward exclusivity that takes social work farther away from the populations that it is allegedly designed to serve. From the pinnacle only the heavens are in view; the teeming masses below are obscured by the clouds.

Still other factors militate against social work education being contained within the university structure: the repetitive aspects of learning in class and field; the overemphasis on teaching aspects that have academic acceptance; the maternalism in the faculty-student relationship; the "busy work" nature of many of the classes; and the difficulty students have in negotiating the complex bureaucratic systems within the school, in negotiating agency systems as well as school systems, and then attempting to negotiate the queasy interrelationship between both systems, all of which is essentially external to the nature of social work—the provision of services to the needy. Small wonder students are "turned off" soon after entry into schools of social work!

Faculty and administration, steeped in analytic techniques, have built-in defense mechanisms to cope with the attacks students mount against educational practice. These attacks are known as the "October revolution"—the dismay being recognized early in the school year—and they refer to the "adolescent rebellion," even though most students are hardly adolescent. The school has evolved a whole system of self-satisfying rationalizations to justify its position and educational stance.

Can reform within the educational system permit social work to emerge as a viable helping force and still maintain its academic knowledge-base and its academic credentials? It does not appear likely. The differences between academic pursuit and the acquisition of practice skills remain largely irreconcilable. As long as the former is and should be the province of the university, then the latter should be accomplished elsewhere. Mere curriculum changes, course additions or subtractions, the reassigning of academic credits, the lengthening or shortening of time in the field, or the host of innovative directions being taken by the social work educational system still revolve around a fundamental bias: that social work is a profession and professions are taught within an academic structure. As long as this remains an unchallenged axiom, social work must *inevitably* be caught up in a system of academic ground rules—scholarly pursuit and academic recognition at the terrible price of demeaning its practice component and its service commitment. Reform does not appear to be feasible as long as these basic contradictions persist. And many times a friendly divorce is preferable to a loveless marriage.

What is being served by the field's espousal of "professionalism?" In 1972, these many years after social work has become dignified by academic recognition, the field still casts about for an "image," an "identification." In a recent issue of *Social Work* (March, 1972), Harry Specht decries "activism" as eroding the social work profession.[11] Quite the contrary, it is professionalism that is eroding activism. It is intellectual pretensions and failure to deliver on its promises that are spelling the doom of social work. Specht and others in the field suggest the separation of social welfare from social work. Gone will be the confusion between the welfare investigator and the social worker. Gone will be the anger of minority groups who see social workers as people who deny them money or meddle in their lives without the knowledge an M.S.W. should give.

Gone, gone, gone. When trouble brews it is the social worker who leaves the scene. Retreat from reality into professionalism. Deny the poor, deny the minorities, deny the social problems—after all, social work didn't create them, did it? Why should it be responsible? Instead, goes the argument, let us focus on the problems social work *has* created—such as defining just what social work is all about.

In the same issue of *Social Work* the following points were made regarding social workers in hospital settings: "Because hospital social workers have little influence on their caseloads, the question has been raised as to whether physicians understand the function of the medical social worker." The author goes on to identify the social services the medical social worker does perform. For whom? For the doctors? No—for the social worker. In another article: ". . . social workers do little more than complain bitterly to each other or to the administrator about their low-level work and their treatment as physician's handmaidens rather than as . . . colleagues." [12]

These are, in brief, the training for dependency: the refusal to deal with issues of moment and the retreat from dealing with social problems. (Leave the welfare institutions, indeed! And go where? And do what? And what about those damned poor souls on welfare?) And then there are the social workers' lamentations about their dependency role—their handmaiden positions with respect to other professions. In essence, this is the problem of social work. Wrapping itself in professionalism, social work stands aloof from service, stands aloof from the poor, stands aloof from social problems, and then bewails the fact that nobody loves it. What reason does anyone have to love it since it is so uncommitted, so blurred in its focus, so unwilling to extricate itself from intellectual hypocrisy?

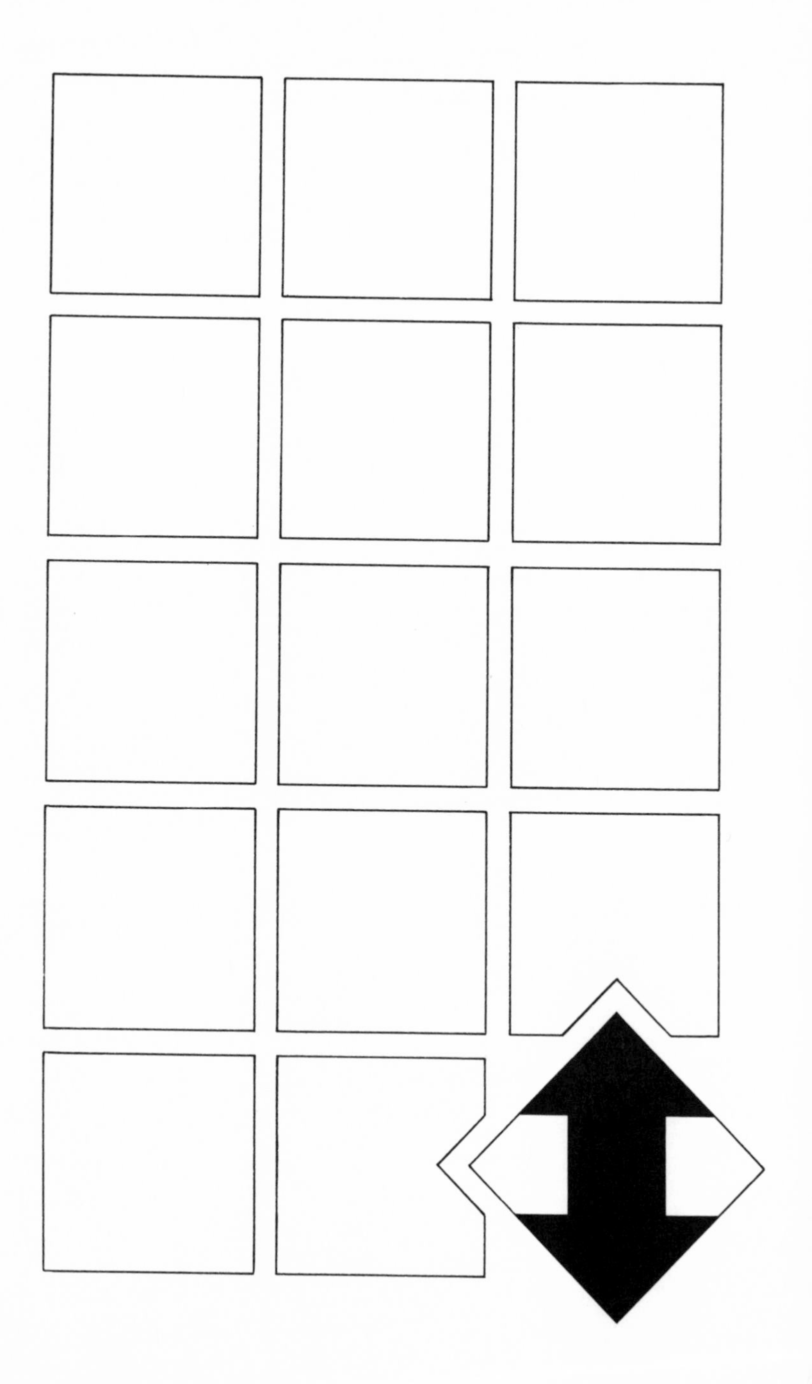

CHAPTER 5
SOCIAL WORK-PRACTICE OR PERISH

The vast majority of social workers practice through agency structures. Indigenous to agency structure is the chain of command, a hierarchy of forces determining policy, services, etc. Upon entering the agency service, the graduate social worker immediately enters into a program of supervision. No other field imposes so much supervision as does social work. While in school, the student social worker receives intensive supervision as part of the discipline's training. For the graduate, fully certified, supervision continues and continues, either for the life of the agency or the life of the social worker.

At times the social worker is promoted to supervisor, wherein he supervises. But supervisors themselves are supervised and so on, ad infinitum. Of course there are cogent reasons for the extent of this supervision, related to the agency structure and the services of the agency in which social work is practiced. But there is an important side effect for the ego of the social worker. He may at some time ask himself at what point he stands on his own feet. At what point is he a professional capable of making his own decisions? At what point is he sufficiently free not to have his work scrutinized and evaluated?

Supervision has many benefits; certainly the knowledge-base through which social workers should be operating is great and ever-expanding and would require literally a lifetime of pursuit. Supervision, however, is an extremely costly process in terms of time. The function of the supervisor in the agency may be only to supervise and administer, but time is necessary for preparation of materials for supervision as well as the time spent in supervision itself.

Supervision is by and large a one-to-one process. The introduction of group supervisory techniques is in its beginning stages throughout the field. Supervision, incidentally, does not necessarily lead to an expansion of the social worker's knowledge-base but may lead to the improvement of the social worker's skills. Once again, however, the skills are usually treatment skills that are reinforced in the supervisory process. The concept of supervision has been developed from the psychotherapeutic model where the therapist receives a period of supervision or consultation before embarking on his own. Whereas the therapist ultimately assumes responsibility for himself and his practice, the social worker does not. Supervision has become a condition of professional life for the social worker and has cast the social worker into a career of dependence.

Social workers are heavily committed to the concept of "conference." Action is rarely planned or executed without the concurrence of a large number of people. The greater the number of participants in the conference the better, and the greater the number of conferences, also the better (the implicit reassurance is that should the plan fail, there is enough shared responsibility so that the guilt will not be borne solely by any one individual). There is an unconscious wish also involved here, that the problem that is being worked on may dissipate during the prolonged schedule of conferences. It sometimes works.

Many of the more prestigious agencies in the field offer in-service training programs for their professional staff. The quality of these programs obviously varies considerably, but again, they mostly appear to be geared to increased understanding of therapeutic skills. Upon graduation many students are attracted to agencies that offer more sophisticated training in those areas that they have been programmed to accept as being social work—more and more sophisticated techniques for reaching a middle-class population.

One cannot be naïve enough to assume a position of

being steadfastly against supervision, conferences, or in-service training. One can raise questions, however, about the balance these factors assume in the practice of social work, the content of these processes, and the pro forma attention they receive. Far too often these practices have become ritualistic, empty of meaningful content, obligatory but not purposeful. The agency structure demands its continued survival, and reinforcement of its view of problems, and the perpetuation of its methods for dealing with the problems it has identified. This is ensured through the processes of supervision, conference, and in-service training. Instances of major change in service delivery, such as those of CSS, are all too rare.

Under this barrage of well-intentioned procedures the professional social worker must question his competence and abilities. He must wonder what little he has received in two years of graduate education that so much more time is needed to teach him. He must wonder about his classification as a professional—is it real? At what point is he qualified to function independently?

Little study has been done on the overall working day of the social worker. Each conference, each supervisory and inservice session, takes time away from practice. One famous time-cost study revealed that out of every $100 the agency was spending for casework services, only $42.49 went for interview costs. The remainder went for such things as case recording, supervisory conferences, and case consultation.[1] Estimates of time spent in actual service or in preparation for service by social workers must vary considerably from agency to agency: further research in this area would be illuminating. By virtue of training and educational bias, social workers move toward the "motivated" client—the middle-class-oriented client seeking help for his emotional problems. It is almost as though the social worker needs the client more than the client the worker! It is precisely this kind of motivated client who validates the efficacy of the training, assuring the social worker that his training and skills are purposeful. The social worker sorely needs this type of reassurance.

The agency further promotes the image of the social worker as inadequate through its systems of accountability, principally through its record-keeping. From the beginning of their training through agency practice, social workers are required to keep extensive written records of their activity. Not only do ethical considerations arise as to the content of the information recorded—what use will the agency make of material?—not only does it require the social worker to expose his practice to an endless host of overseeing forces; but time devoted to record-keeping can be enormous.

Part of the insecurity of the social worker, and his anger as well, results from the inordinate amount of effort invested in the written word. Language has been briefly mentioned before, but again their records and reports are labored, repetitive, and obscure. In some manner the written records have become validations of the social worker's existence—their weight and length have at times become acute administrative problems.

Consider the social worker in agency practice. He is supervised; he is in ongoing training; he is in perpetual conference, he has administrative functions, and if in this plethora of activities he chances to see a client, he must record the activity, which in itself leads to an increasing round of supervision, conference, scheduling, and so on. It is not only the high caseloads to which caseworkers are assigned that lead to their many frustrations, but it is also the ancillary work, which implies a lack of trust in their competency.

His own training has ill prepared the social worker for the realities of work. The agency structure mistrusts his competence. He himself feels impotent in the face of the crushing realities of his clients' lives (there is that vague feeling that what he is doing is not what it is all about, but that it is a ritual *about* what it is all about). The overlay of psychoanalytic jargon and the euphemisms of social-workese may suppress the doubts but rarely do they extinguish them. The social worker is indeed a creature of conflicts.

At the beginning of the present century the social worker, like the itinerant peddler, had a plethora of services to offer his clients. Here were food, clothing, and cookingware; here were tangible goods and concrete services. And at the same time he could be the friendly ear, the counselor, the educator, the old friend, the advocate, and even the social reformer if this was what the needs of the people he was serving dictated. The work of the social worker was not determined by any particular bias or a priori commitment on his part, but was based on the circumstances and needs of his clients. ". . . He seemed to know that no single function could be adequate to meet the array of problems his client brought to him." [2]

In *Social Diagnosis,* written in the early twentieth century, Mary Richmond said, "Social casework may be defined as the art of doing different things for and with different people by cooperating with them to achieve at one and the same time their own and society's betterment." This simple statement contrasts sharply with today's obscure analytic definitions.

With the growing commitment to and obsession with Freud in the mid-1930's, social work took an enormous step toward its present predicament. For here was presented a new dimension of man—the unconscious—to be probed and explored as a determinant force in his life.

Freud served social work in several crucial ways. He offered a modus operandi for dealing with people. He prescribed how to probe the unconscious and how to cope with anxieties, repressions, and defense mechanisms. By explaining and clarifying the inner psychic world, he provided the beginnings of a technique for helping people in distress. He also provided social work with an identity—the very recognition with professional overtones that social work felt it so sorely lacked. This desperate search for professional identification has preoccupied social workers, both before the Freudian era and in the years since. The arguments for its professionalism sound just as shrill today in academic debate and in the professional literature. Social work attempts to attain professional status by a dictionary definition of "profession," not by its contribution to society and not by its practice.

The Freudian prescription offered social work a way out of a tangled dilemma that might have had awkward repercussions. If social work was to deal directly with those social conditions that produced poverty, sooner or later it would have to look critically at society itself —at the entire system that produced, for example, the intense human tragedy of the ghetto. Whether the system would tolerate this criticism and continue to fund and recognize social work is doubtful.

Thus Freud offered social work a solution, a way to reduce its radicalizing potential by focusing on man himself and his unconscious while studiously ignoring all other forces. Social work was saved! This new and challenging dimension of man became a therapeutic obsession, perfectly acceptable to the Establishment. Also, social workers were being genuinely helpful by offering people relief from emotional distress. Also the field had finally found professional respectability; it was now "recognized." Ultimately, Freudianism became a near-fatal diversion, siphoning away the field's creative energies from people in desperate need of social service—the poor and disadvantaged.

Until very recently, then, the "service for the welfare of mankind" was directed toward liberating the emotional resources of man. As opposed to the social worker at the turn of the century, the modern social worker is provided with a "point of view," a frame of reference, and a therapeutic approach to his client. The modern social worker is less prepared to assume a multitude of roles with his client than his predecessors were. His expertise lies in his ability to identify and alleviate the emotional distress of his client.

This is not to say that the psychotherapeutic position is invalid. It becomes invalid, however, when an inordinate amount of time and attention is paid it, to the neglect of all other forces and social conditions that influence man. The additional training the social worker receives in practice from his agency continues to reflect and emphasize this narrow definition of role. The development of his psychotherapeutic expertise is deemed most important. One never hears, for example, of an economist brought in for the in-service training of social workers in an agency. While Freud has given social work the illusion of a respectable role, he has also truncated that role, perhaps fatally.

While the rhetoric of social work continues to insist that the social worker is an intervener in social forces, and the public image of the social worker continues to be that of the dedicated but determined worker, plodding through slums and streets of poverty, the realities of social work education and practice are altogether different. The world of the social worker is the world of inner structures: the ego, id, and superego; of repressions; defense mechanisms; neurotic conflicts; anxieties; and the Oedipal myth. It is an office-oriented world—not street-oriented. It is a world of *reacting* to and not *acting upon* social realities. The outer world of the social environment, consisting of economic systems, cultural forces, and social classes, is as alien to the social worker as the geography of Jupiter.

Interestingly enough, this inner world of psychic forces is less susceptible to change than the outer environmental world. Only by dint of monumental psychotherapeutic efforts that consume vast amounts of resources, time, money, and manpower can beneficial change be expected. On the other hand, social conditions are more the product of man's conscious rather than unconscious design. Consider the wide variety of social systems extant in the world today. And, while social conditions are also highly resistant to modifications, they are still more demonstrably amenable to change.

Unlike the inner realities that remain relatively fixed no matter where one stands on the planet, social realities are in a constant state of flux. The work, the energy, and the time involved in alleviating the internal distress of a single individual or of a small group of individuals are largely unproductive, since this is the area least amenable to change. Why did social work devote most of its energies to this arena and for all practical purposes abdicate the arena of social realities?

The reasons are simple: by doing so it has wittingly or unwittingly played directly into the hands of those whose interest lies in preserving the social relationships and power positions as they exist today—in preserving the status quo.

The help social workers offer to the individual today consists of enabling them to make internal adjustments to existing realities. For some segments of the population, primarily the middle class, intervention of this sort *may* indeed alleviate personal and interfamilial pressures. *May,* because there are varying schools of thought and varying methods of approach, usually determined by the school one attended. Scott Briar argues that while a caseworker *may* have some knowledge of a particular theory of personality, his knowledge is generally limited to that theory, and "in other areas of psychology he may be no better informed than the layman." [3]

For others, for the people who usually fall at the lower ends of the economic scale, this approach is less than meaningless. This type of intervention presupposes that the poor themselves and not the conditions of social existence are responsible for their difficulties. This is a contemporary version of the puritanical creed that poverty is the result of a person's moral shortcomings, now modernized and couched in sophisticated psychoanalytic terminology but still parboiled Puritanism. The fundamental belief here promulgated is that it is man's duty to adjust to the system, rather than the system's responsibility to meet the needs of man.

By lending professional credence to this view, by pointing the finger at man as the guilty party, the social worker helps prop up the system in bad times and good. The individual is then a straw man who gives the social worker something to do but whose hidden purpose is to divert energies from where they are needed most and so to permit social unjustices to continue unabated.

There must be a law, analogous to the physical law of water seeking its own level, which, simply stated, would be that all the benefits available to man will sooner or later be siphoned off and channeled to those who need them least. How else can one account for social workers performing psychoanalytic services in the ghetto? How else can one account for the Bureau of Child Guidance—the treatment arm of the Board of

Education in New York—working with motivated candidates for psychotherapy and deserting the masses of the poor children who can't adjust to the school system?

Social work's initial idealistic impetus was directed toward serving those who had the greatest need for the services provided. When social work discovered Freud and entered the chase for professional status, its idealism was lost. Perhaps it would have been more honest at that point for social work to think out its rhetoric anew—even recast its professional title, changing it from "social work" to "psychiatric therapy" or "therapeutic work." These at least reflect the actual work it performs. What has happened very simply is that social work has left the area of greatest need for the areas of lesser need. It has abandoned the poor for the suburbs.

Social work has not developed methods for reaching out to the poor—those large masses in our society who have the most need for service—nor, unfortunately, has it shown any genuine inclination to develop these methods. With the discovery of Freud, all benefits flowed upward rather than downward. Social work has been doing more and more for fewer and fewer because this is the road to professional respectability. Social work was admitted to the universities as a "profession," eligible for academic status, the conferring of degrees, and all the other time-honored prerogatives of respectability.

The Establishment has mandated social work to "keep the lid on"; that is, to maintain the status quo. Therapeutic intervention disturbs the equilibrium of the individual, his family, and perhaps a friend or two, but as far as the broader aspects of society are concerned, it is safe medicine. Other kinds of intervention, however, may not be quite as safe and will pose too many latent threats to the established order. These tinker dangerously with the distribution of goods and power and pose a distinct threat to the uneasy balance that exists today between the haves and the have-nots.

One can look with suspicion on the heavy investment society has made in the area of social work through its support of various agencies, its financing of training units, and the granting of scholarships and stipends for social work training. Is maintainance of the status quo implied in this support? Whatever the reasons, social workers *do* deal with potential threats to the established order of things. However, the manner in which they have chosen to do their business has been one that poses no threat to the current social system of balances.

If radicalized, the poor could indeed represent a serious threat to the social, political, and economic order of society. The very existence of that threat could well ensure a more even distribution of society's resources. Since social work's major thrust does not attempt to alter the conditions that create the poor, and since it delivers just enough to meet the basic needs for survival of the poor, it can be argued that social work practice tends to deradicalize the poor.

As illustrative of this, note how social work deals with the problems of so-called disturbed youth. In popular terms they are referred to as juvenile delinquents, the gangs that were quite prevalent in urban centers particularly during the 1960's. They had their "turf" and their internecine warfare. They would mug people, steal cars, commit burglary, and in many ways threaten the balance of their communities; the drug addicts of today have a similar relationship to the local population. Social work made some attempts to "work with" these gangs in the community, but all too often the treatment of choice became isolation from the community. Isolation from the community meant placement in residential homes for the emotionally disturbed or confinement in training schools. In actuality, residential treatment and training schools provided an artificial environment. Successful adaptation led to the return of the individual to the very same environmental conditions that caused the problem in the first place. These institutions, very costly to run, have been well-documented failures; their recidivism rates have been appalling.

These gangs have changed form—not because of psychotherapeutic intervention, but from their own increased awareness of social action as an instrument of self-help. They moved from random destruction and self-defeating acts of aggression to specific social actions attempting concrete gains for their people; better medical services, hot breakfasts for poor school children, lower prices for food, and so forth. These are not the practice techniques of social work. Social action, political organization, direct confrontation, and implied terror are not the ways of the social worker. And because these are not social workers' ways, the poor have abandoned them and are evolving their own programs of political and social welfare.

Too rigid, too ossified, too "professional" in their stance to truly reexamine their methods of practice, social workers have been routed from the action. They have left the street for the office, the real community for the artificial community, and, aside from a beep about an "advocacy" role, they have surrendered their function as spokesmen for the oppressed. The social worker is deeply distressed about what he is supposed to do. Since he has not "made it" with the poor, he is turning closer to the Establishment for a role definition

—manpower management and middle-line administration concepts are being promoted in the professional journals.

This "function" crisis social work is going through at this time is not only related to the fact that social work has failed in its contract with the poor. It has also failed in its contract with the Establishment: it has failed to maintain the order that society has deemed essential for its own survival.

By entering into this contract in the first place, social work has traded off some of its humanity for respectability. Perhaps this was the only way for it to survive.

What, if anything, can be done? Must this profession be written off? If there is any way out of the present-day morass, it has to be found quickly. And the surgery required is major.

Stop the nonsense and get back into the business of doing things for people. To accomplish this there has to be a reordering of existing priorities. Rather than the schools of social work being the determinants of practice, put practice determination where it belongs: back in the community.

Rather than having schools of social work, have practice centers, educational enclaves, or satellites located in the streets. These small groups would be located in areas of greatest need (ghettos, poverty pockets) where experienced social workers and beginning social workers could have easy access. These learning centers would be run by practitioners chosen by the community, the workers, and the students. Since these centers would be open to all people in the community regardless of training and background, the distinctions between clients, workers, and students would hopefully be so blurred as to make them indistinguishable from one another.

There would be no curriculum in these centers. They would be focused on the problems of the community in which they were located. Learning would emerge from coping with needs, from searching for solutions to the community problems. Learning would be group centered—a mutual sharing by all concerned. These centers would be used freely by both the community and the students.

The university complex—not the schools of social work per se—would serve as the educational back-up for these satellite training centers. Courses and content would be selected on the basis of the needs of the community enclave. One or two members would be picked to take these courses and report the material back to the enclave, thus making it available to all and not just to those few taking the course. If political expertise is needed, for example, a course in political science may be helpful—or a meeting with the mayor or another political figure. The important thing is that all institutions of the society would serve community needs and the enclave would reach out to all of them for potential solutions to their problems. Whatever knowledge or information is gained thus becomes shared and is not retained as it is in the elitist concept.

Under this plan, schools of social work would be eliminated or would serve only in a narrow administrative capacity as a referral source for specific learning needs. Perhaps they can function as a certifying body for the social workers so produced, but only after a major overhaul of criteria and standards is effected.

These are only the bare outlines of a program that, if implemented, may still not save social work. Hopefully though, it would open the field to all the poor and the ghettoized. This program would serve to eliminate the elitism that separates social work from the poor. It would create an *independent* social worker who would be trained to challenge rather than accept social realities and to fight where fight is indicated. It would put social work back in the community it should never have left. It would open up areas of practice presently eschewed by professional leadership, such as political action, mobilization, etc. As long as social work remains in the streets where it belongs, practice—not academic skills—will emerge as paramount.

The "we" and "they" attitude that divides practitioners and clients and that current social work education reinforces deserves to be ended. As any good social worker knows, people are much more alike than they are different. Social workers *are* people. Professionalism, that pretense to a unique expertise, and its concomitant specialization—in short, the whole academic paraphernalia—serve to reinforce the difference between the social worker and his client. This luxury social work can no longer afford.

SECTION 3
THE CASE FOR REFORM—THE EMERGENCE OF A NEW PROFESSIONALISM

Walking into the office for the first time, he tried to keep his back straight. A small man with a faint moustache, he let his head hang slightly downward and he cast his eyes furtively from side to side as he entered. The waiting room was crowded with people scattered in rows of folding chairs, as though waiting for a movie to start. For the most part they were unnaturally quiet with their heads bowed and their eyes shut or staring vacantly into nothingness. One man was sprawled, half-sliding from his chair, reeking of alcohol and snoring loudly. Children—some black, others tow-haired—played loudly, their faces dirty and their clothing ill-fitting. Infants were sleeping in their mothers' arms; one bronze baby was sucking eagerly. A small girl with round eyes and a stained white dress, biting on her thumb, watched him as he entered.

A sharp smell of disinfectant filled his nostrils as he entered. Here, too, this Monday morning, the floor had been disinfected for the arrival of the new applicants, the old-timers, the petitioners—those suing, the misfits, and the plain out-and-out hungry. The pale green paint was peeling from the walls. The waiting room was overlit with harsh fluorescence that laid bare all things —all wrinkles, all blemishes, all secrets. There was no place to hide under the pitiless glare that cast no shadow. Again the contrast with the factory, ill-lit and shadowed and whirring with sewing machines and flying lint and bits of cloth—where a man could hide his head—even though it was dirty—where he could keep a private thought. A sign on the wall warned him in English and his native Spanish that he should not smoke. But ash trays were scattered around, filled with butts and caked with ancient cigarette ash.

"Can I help you?" The voice was tired. There was a muted sound of wanting to help, but she did not look up as she wrote on papers.

"Yes, please . . . I have no job . . . my wife . . . my children . . . the landlord he. . . ." He was lapsing into Spanish, although he was proud of the English he had learned so quickly. And the speech that he had prepared as he walked the ten blocks to the welfare center, the speech that would explain his plight with dignity, his request, had fled him.

"Have you ever received public assistance before?" she interrupted.

He was confused. Public assistance? He stared at her blankly, hearing his brain tumbling and feeling his face redden.

"Welfare," she said patiently. "Have you ever been on welfare?" She was a young black woman; pretty, efficient. Her desk was cluttered with papers, important papers—forms, printing, with little boxes, with lines filled in, with mimeographed signatures and seals, with words that said "I swear . . ." and "I promise . . ." and "it is certified that. . . ," none of which he could read, but all of which were official.

He shook his head. No. No. No welfare. Never. Shame. Shame. NO. Never.

"Your name?"

He told her, quietly.

"I can't hear you."

Louder. Some of the people turned to look at him. One lady was smiling. She understood his shame and it amused her. The little girl with the dirty white dress stared owlishly at him, her thumb still in her mouth.

He told her his name again and she wrote it down.

"Where do you live?"

She checked his address against a list, then bit her lip with a small anger.

"O.K. Sit down. A caseworker will talk to you."

"Please . . . por favor . . . I have no job . . . I. . . ."

"Please sit down over there," she grunted, "a caseworker will see you soon."

He moved to a chair, as far away from the others as possible. The lady who had been smiling at him was still smiling at him. She is crazy, he thought. That is all she can do is smile. He fought the flush that he felt mounting to his temples and sat down. It grew quiet. The children had disappeared. People had come in. People had left. An old school clock on the wall was ticking insistently. Behind the walls of the waiting room he could hear the snapping of a typewriter and a busy hum of muted voices. He dozed. The room was warm. He jerked awake from time to time, glancing around the room. The people had all changed. The girl in the dirty white dress had gone. Only the smiling woman was still here. She was staring at the clock, still smiling. She must be very happy, he thought, to have something to smile about.

"Ramón García! Ramón García!"

He started from his doze. They were calling him. He was panicked. What should he do? Should he put up his hand? Should he stand up? Should he walk to the voice? What? What?

"Ramón García!"

He wanted to put his jacket over his head and run from the building.

"Ramón García!" Irritated now, angry. The man who called his name leaned over the girl behind the desk.

He kept his head down. His name, flung around the room, bounced off the walls. Ramón García. Ramón García. You welfare, you! Ramón García! His name went screaming through the building, out the windows, and down to the streets! Ramón García! Ramón García! Now they all know. All of them. He shut his eyes and clenched his fists and kept his head down.

"Mr. García?"

The man was tapping him on the shoulder. He nodded.

"Please come with me."

He got up and followed the man's shoes. Every head in the room he knew was watching him, every eye in the building was on him. All work had stopped. No tapping typewriters. No muted voices. Ramón García Welfare. His face burned fire. The President in his big house in Washington stopped putting his name to big piles of paper and said, "Ramón García Welfare," and shook his head in disgust.

The caseworker led him down a long hall and took him into a little room. There was no door to the room, and people passing along the corridor could look in on him. In addition, the walls on the little room did not go to the ceiling but only halfway up, so every word he said could be heard, even by the smiling woman who was crazy but happy and who still sat in the waiting room.

He sat on another folding chair and tried to make himself even smaller. The caseworker was a big man, much bigger than him, much bigger than any man he had ever seen, much bigger than a giant, his body overflowed the chair, his head brushed the ceiling. When he bent over to talk to him his face filled the whole cubicle.

"You speak English?" The voice was thunder, bouncing off his ears.

He nodded. He wanted to say, "I speak very well English," in a loud voice with no trace of an accent. He wanted to, but he hung his head and he nodded.

"Good."

Was it?

"Now I want to ask you some questions." He put a form on the desk. It was a long form running five thousand pages. And the questions began. The caseworker wrote down everything he said. Wrote it down on the form. At first his replies were inaudible and the case-

worker had to repeat the questions. Then he was able to speak louder, but he did not know the answers to many of the questions. They were strange questions, many of them. They had nothing to do with the fact that there was no food in the house. That Ramón, Jr., had no milk. That he had a big piece of paper in his pocket that was written in big type that said "Whereas . . ." and told him that if the rent weren't paid, they would put him and his family into the street or. . . .

"And what is the date of your birth?"

"1934."

"And the month?"

"April."

"And the day?"

"17th."

"Where were you born?"

"In Puerto Rico."

"Where in Puerto Rico?"

"Ponce."

"Do you have a birth certificate?"

"I do not know."

"When did you come to New York?"

"Eight . . . maybe ten years. . . ."

"Do you remember exactly?"

"I do not know." They will not help me—I do not know.

"What are the birthdates of your children?"

His mind reeled. He could not remember.

"When did your mother die? What work did your father do? Who are your relatives? Where do they live? Are you a veteran? Did you get U.I.B.?"

"U.I.B.?"

"Unemployment Insurance Benefits."

"How long have you worked there? And before that? And before that? How far in school did you go? Do you

have a bank account? Life insurance? Do you have any other resources?"

"Resources?"

"Anything worth any money?

"No. No."

"How much money did you make?"

"How much is your rent?"

"Do you have any receipts?"

He wrote it all down. Sometimes he asked questions. Maybe he doesn't believe me. Yes. No. I don't know. Maybe that is why the lady was smiling. She knows. He shrank still further into his chair. He was soaked in perspiration. He rubbed his hands along his pants to dry his palms.

"Why are you applying for Public . . . Welfare?"

At last! He would tell him. He had no money. His wife, his children—they were hungry. The landlord—he. . . .

He started to tell him. He was confused. He started in Spanish: "Soy muy. . . ." He stopped. His English? Where was his English? Inglés! Inglés! The man was waiting, tapping his pencil on the desk. Welfare! Welfare! Mama! The President. . . . He began to cry.

"Someone will be out to see you," the caseworker was saying, "within twenty-four hours."

"See me? But the landlord . . . ?"

He had shown the caseworker the piece of paper. It was folded within his pocket. Folded four times to preserve it. The caseworker had carefully unfolded it on his desk, smoothing out the creases as he did so. Whereas. . . .

"A dispossess notice. Nothing to worry about. . . ."

"My family in the street. . . ."

"Nothing to worry about until you get an eviction notice. . . ."

"Can you . . . help me . . . my family?"

"We'll have to investigate."

"Investigate?"

"Investigate. Someone will be out tomorrow."

"Tomorrow?"

"Yes, someone must go out within twenty-four hours."

"I have . . . no food. . . ." Must I beg?

"Surely you can get someone to help you—until tomorrow?"

"Sí." He closed his eyes. They were burning with shame.

"Just sign the application, Mr. García."

He took a firm grip on the pen. His hands were trembling and he wrote his name very slowly and very poorly. The caseworker led him back to the waiting room. The smiling woman was gone.

CHAPTER 6
A DIFFERENT BREED

For the thousands of Mr. Garcías—as well as the millions of taxpayers and politicians who begrudge him his quest for a bit of dignity and sustenance—public welfare is the beginning and end of social work; paradoxically, social workers tend to shun public welfare as a career. These sprawling bureaucracies represent not so much social work in action as the system that social workers could never conquer. There is no institution on which the professional community has expended more rhetoric and more of its reformist activity. And still the Garcías get the last ounce of humanity squeezed out of them by the system. The failure to influence welfare policies to any great degree is nothing new for social work professionals. What *is* relatively new is their candor in admitting the failure. But with the candor has come a pervasive sense of pessimism.

These have been good years for pessimists. It is easy to see social work as a dying institution, destined to be unmourned in death as it has been unloved in life. But while there *is* much in social work that is hardly worth saving, there is that creative spark that has persisted throughout the history of the field, however dimly at times. And in recent years that spark has been burning more brightly—not always to the satisfaction of social workers seeking to return to a quieter time in the life of the profession.

One mark of any fundamental change is the fact that people caught in the midst of it frequently do not realize it is happening or else that they grossly misread its significance. This tendency is not without its uses, for it allows a system to pretend that things are as they were. Those who have a vested interest in protecting the old order can go on about their business undisturbed, believing that whatever minor distractions are occurring will pass away, leaving the "tested truths" intact. For those who are unhappy with the old order, the belief that nothing is changing allows for much handwringing and breastbeating—and a minimum of concrete action either to alter the system or to replace it.

In view of the major crisis in social work today, it is striking to what extent the social workers—both optimists and pessimists—are treating the whole process as a temporary lapse in an otherwise changeless order. The clinician whose mind is glued firmly to what Freud said more than half a century ago has seen the urban crisis come and go, and he feels vindicated by the shift to the right in the body politic. We can now go back to the business of emulating the established entrepreneurial professions. This step backward is now being institutionalized in the form of the societies for clinical social work that have sprung up around the country. Their backbone is the private practitioner and his quasi-private counterparts in various treatment settings. Their agenda is the licensing of social workers —to keep out the "unqualified"—and the infusion of social work curricula with less social action and more psychoanalytic psychology.

But many social workers who yearn for a profession more attuned to the strivings of the poor and alienated and better able to influence social policy are equally oblivious to the fundamental changes going on in social work. Having seen their brightest hopes ground down by the forces of reaction, they are ready to believe that social work is destined forever to remain the minion of entrenched social welfare bureaucracies.

The fact is that social work *is* changing and changing drastically. Events are moving beyond the control of the self-appointed guardians of stability. Having seen an image of something better, a growing number of minority social workers, young workers in the field, and social work students are not content to settle back into the old rut. They are demanding a different kind of profession. And, oddest of all, the professional leadership is listening.

Many social workers remain oblivious to what is going on. Others want to move with the new tempo but are unable to. Their situation is perhaps most tragic, for they sense the crisis and yet are not able to make the transition. Such a social worker is a person we shall call Harriet North.

Harriet started out as a schoolteacher, then decided that social work would be a more meaningful career. After receiving her master's degree from the University of Chicago in the early 1950's, she landed a choice job as a psychiatric caseworker in one of the foremost child guidance clinics in the country.

In a few years Harriet moved up to become a supervisor—unusual in that agency for one with her limited experience. It wasn't long before she began supervising social work students in their field work, a key part of their training. Then a significant mark of recognition came from her profession: a paper she gave at a conference was accepted for publication in the leading social work journal.

Harriet North led two lives, really, both wrapped up in the social work profession. Unlike most of her colleagues in the clinic, she was also active in the social action committee of the local chapter of the National Association of Social Workers. One could always count on Harriet to write letters to her congressman or to join the delegation to see the mayor's staff. It troubled her that these were really two separate worlds, the one teeming with important political figures and an atmosphere of controversy, and the other immersed in the psychoanalytic mystique. It was as if she were really two different persons.

It was in 1961 that Harriet North brought her two worlds together. Inspired by President Kennedy's appeal to social conscience, Harriet left the glamor of the child guidance clinic for a grubby little cubicle on the third floor of the former warehouse that housed the central office of the county welfare department. She became the director of a project that was to provide intensive services to welfare recipients.

At first it was exciting and rewarding. The young caseworkers in her unit believed in her and in their clients and themselves. Harriet was sought out for informal consultation by old-line workers. She even came to relish the sparring with the welfare director—a political hack who hated social workers, clients, and blacks with equal fervor.

Then things started to go wrong for Harriet North. It began with the young doctoral graduate—a relative rarity in social work at the time—who was hired to evaluate her program. He obviously didn't care about people, only statistics. He sneered at casework and said Freud was bunk. And he continually seemed to twist what Harriet and her workers said about their work so that it always came out sounding negative. She found herself lying awake at night thinking up answers to the hostile questions he would fire at her the next day. He finally left the project, and the research director of the local health and welfare council managed to put together an evaluation of sorts—primarily a string of case anecdotes.

By this time a new breed of caseworkers—aggressive and challenging—was beginning to appear around the agency. One young girl who insisted on wearing jeans and sandals found her way into Harriet's unit. When asked to dress differently, she accused Harriet of being irrelevant and out of touch, sprinkling her lecture with a few well-chosen four-letter words. The new social work graduates seemed to be bent on attacking the agency, attacking social work, and inciting clients to make trouble. At least with the whites Harriet felt she could talk the same language. But she found the sullenness and anger of young black workers and client leaders incomprehensible. This hurt because Harriet had always prided herself on good relations with all races, and she had fought fiercely in behalf of school integration and open housing.

More and more, Harriet North found herself defending—defending herself, her profession, and her agency. In fact, it was a little hard to distinguish between these three at times. Her profession had long since become her life. And the agency had become the central core—the set of givens—around which her professional life revolved. It had started years before, when her graduate training focused more than anything else around her field work experiences under the tutelage of agency supervisors.

The last straw came when a committee of the local chapter of the National Association of Social Workers issued a report that was critical of Harriet's agency, including her own project. Public welfare workers had long been accustomed to barbs from conservatives and tax-minded legislators, but this attack used the same rhetoric Harriet had been hearing from the young activists. She tried to resign from the professional association but discovered she was trapped by insurance benefits she could not afford to give up. Beaten and disillusioned, she now holds on to her job and her shrinking circle of colleagues as the only ties with her profession, waiting for the day she can retire.

Harriet North's story is a tragedy, partly because she never understood the larger issues in which she was enmeshed. She was a pawn in a struggle between newly emerging forces and a social welfare industry incapable of responding, one that had become brutal and dehumanizing. Harriet devoted her professional life to that industry, only to become one of its victims. The other tragedy is that Harriet has misperceived the real enemy. The young black and white activists appeared to be bent on destroying the social work profession. In reality, they can be its redemption.

Harriet North's inner turmoil symbolizes the turmoil in the social work profession today. It is not only middle-aged matrons who are having trouble connecting with the rapid changes in the field. Young people drawn by the fascination of intensive therapy, careerists who see their hard-earned rewards and recognition eroded between an angry clientele and a vindictive majority—all these are having trouble responding to the new cadence of change in the profession.

The Harriet Norths are not all there is to social work. In recent years a new breed of social worker has appeared, a social worker reminiscent of the early settlement house residents who fought injustice side by side with immigrants three-quarters of a century ago.

When the Alameda County Welfare Department launched Operation Weekend in the winter of 1963, most of the staff went along. The idea was ingenious and straight out of "Dragnet," with the caseworkers operating in pairs. Striking in the early hours on Sunday mornings, one caseworker would use his "professional relationship" with his client to gain entry to her home. He would then go immediately to the back door to admit his co-worker who was posted there to prevent escape in case the lady's boyfriend was hiding there. Then the two would conduct a top-to-bottom search for the legendary "man in the house." (Aid to Families with Dependent Children is for families without a male breadwinner. So, inverting the principle of innocent until proven guilty, welfare departments start with the presumption that their AFDC clients are cheating—living in sin and collecting welfare checks while a hidden boyfriend brings in a paycheck.)

Many workers found the whole idea repugnant, but only three actually refused to be party to the scheme. Two workers quit rather than participate. Benny Parrish just refused. When the department fired him, he appealed to the Alameda County Civil Service Commission on the grounds that he could not be forced to engage in an unconstitutional action. Not surprisingly, the appeal was turned down. That would have been more than enough for most social workers. Assuming they had refused to act like secret police in the first place, it would have been more characteristic of them simply to leave the department for that mythical "good" agency. Certainly once the Civil Service Commission gave its predictable assent to the firing, it would have made sense to most social workers to "accept reality" and go elsewhere. In the early 1960's it wasn't that hard to find jobs in the manpower-starved welfare field. But Benny Parrish instead took his case to the Superior Court. Almost a year after the firing, the Superior Court upheld the decision.[1]

Despite these setbacks, Parrish had already achieved some important things for poor people far beyond Alameda County; the uproar over his firing had led the Welfare Department to cancel a second Operation Weekend; the California State Department of Public Welfare issued new regulations designed to give a modicum of protection to welfare clients; and, most important, the case had attracted national attention to the growing problem of "midnight raids." [2]

Benny Parrish did not give up. He took his appeal to the California Supreme Court and was finally ordered reinstated. But now it was 1967, more than four years after the original firing.[3] Those four years are not accidental. They are part of a system that can afford to wait out trouble-makers like Benny Parrish, people who don't have the resources to persist, let alone the money to wage protracted legal battles. Benny Parrish could not have done it alone; he won only because social workers and their friends throughout the country rallied around in one of those rare displays of unity.

Benny Parrish was not a graduate of a school of social work, yet he symbolizes what is *right* about social work today. Is it merely an ironic coincidence that he lacked the academic credentials of the social work profession, while Harriet North not only had them but was also helping students gain them? Or is there something about social work education that turns committed young people into unquestioning functionaries?

No, there *are* professional social workers—a new breed of professionals—who have their eyes open to the issues they are involved in and who are not afraid to act in response to what they see. Take Bill Berkan, for instance. In 1970, Berkan was fired from his job as social services director in Adams County, Wisconsin. He was praised by the State Personnel Board as a "competent" administrator who "created order out of the chaotic administration he inherited." His crime? He had fought the County Welfare Board's attempts to cut costs by cutting out vital benefits for clients. In Berkan's words: "The community wished to help the 'worthy,' while I wished to help those in need."

Berkan appealed his dismissal to the State Personnel Board. The board turned down his appeal, on grounds that the local jurisdiction had a right to have the welfare director it wanted. Berkan continued his fight with the solid backing of local and national units of the National Association of Social Workers. The issue has landed in the courts, with the ultimate outcome still up in the air.[4]

Not all professional social workers are like Harriet North. Nor are all nonprofessionals committed champions of the underdog. There are too many callous and punitive nonprofessionals in social agencies to allow us to make that kind of generalization. Although social work's advances in theoretical sophistication have been purchased at a high price in responsiveness and relevancy, in a real sense professionalism—which has helped to make social work precious and introspective and irrelevant in the past—is capable of saving it. There is no middle way in this, for part of professionalism is dying; either social work will die with it or adopt a new kind of professionalism that is bold and exciting.

Most criticisms of professionalism in social work are the same ones leveled at professionalism in general. Professions develop special language systems and secret codes to distinguish the "ins" from the "outs." Professions get state authorities to grant them monopoly control over a sector of work.

Professions make a fetish of prolonged education —with a generous admixture of hokum in most fields. And there is pressure on all professions to act as if they were "sure"—this aura is encouraged as a means of instilling confidence in the clientele. Professional ethics are strongly slanted to protect the members from retaliation outside and fratricide within. Then there is specialization. As general educational levels keep rising in this country, the professions must keep creating elites within elites. So the once-revered general practitioner becomes the poor cousin, and the specialists create subspecialties that eventually will have to find subsubspecialties of their own.

Social work needs to understand how other professions have come to distort their high ethical callings and become ingrown and self-aggrandizing, in order to avoid following in their footsteps. A strong professional community is the only potential countervailing force against continued dominance by the social welfare industry. But the very mechanisms by which social workers can forge such a professional community are also those that can allow it to become another American Medical Association, fending off social justice and institutional change in order to protect its members' material interests.

A new breed of professionals? Watch them at work. It is five in the afternoon—time for the sprawling welfare bureaucracies and chic treatment agencies to call it a day and close their doors. In a rundown part of Long Beach, California, the day is just starting for the Long Beach Free Clinic. In the tiny waiting room a radio pours forth rock music from the local underground station. The street people sit or stand wherever they can find space, waiting to be helped. Soon they are spilling over onto the sidewalk—a fact that will eventually bring complaints from neighbors and force the Free Clinic to find new quarters. But the clinic staff is too busy to worry about that—or the unmarked police car whose occupants suspiciously watch the proceedings.

The services range from medical care for venereal disease and pregnancies to legal assistance, draft counseling, and group and individual therapy. The clinic lives up to its name, for it is free not only in the sense of requiring no payment but also because it is free of the straitjacketed mentality of professional specialization. And its young clients feel free because they don't have to give their names or go through an interrogation to get help. The counseling sometimes goes on in the street outside of the clinic because there is no room inside.

The street people don't mind the inconvenience, because they feel the clinic staff is with them. In the words of one patient: "I've never been to a place like this. I feel I'm as good as anybody else—in spite of my stink." In fact, it is not always easy to tell the staff from clients, because some people from the street have been trained to interview medical patients.[5]

But there is more to this kind of clinic program than meets the eye. Those counselors are professional: they are drawing upon professional expertise when they help a girl decide what to do about an unwanted pregnancy or when they bring a group together to rap about their drug problems. These are complicated problems, and a well-intentioned but untrained helper can quickly get in over his head. These clinic professionals know much more about what they are doing than did their counterparts in the early days of the social settlements, and they have managed to throw off the bureaucratic constrictions and superficial trappings of professionalism that make so many social workers ineffectual these days.

The Long Beach Free Clinic lived a tenuous existence, its survival dependent upon a tiny trickle of funds and the good graces of the police, the medical profession, and city officialdom. That is the story of most such innovative operations. In particular, those whose livelihood has depended on government funds have constantly been in danger of losing their financial base. And the more daring are chronically embroiled in controversy.

The Free Clinic avoided serious reprisals because it concentrated on personal services. But those programs that have taken on the power structure directly have been in constant trouble and have had a short life expectancy.

Lincoln Hospital is located in the most depressed part of the Bronx in New York City. Amidst the turmoil of the 1960's, Lincoln Hospital sought to develop a community mental health program that would be relevant to the real needs of area residents. The Neighborhood Service Center program was one of the results. Operating out of storefronts, it was staffed primarily by community residents trained and supervised by professional social workers. The concept of mental health had to be interpreted very broadly. Federal funds and hospital hierarchies might be packaged according to professional and bureaucratic domain, but people's troubles refused to be so neatly categorized. The people brought all kinds of problems to the storefronts, some related directly to personal funtioning, but more involving encounters with education and health and welfare bureaucracies—*especially* welfare.

It quickly became evident that retail social work, whittling away one case at a time, could never hope to deal with the basic forces creating the problems. The social workers did not ignore those personal crises; to have done so would have destroyed their credibility with their clients. But they also began organizing to take on the established institutions directly. Social workers, community mental health workers, and clients banded together to work for reform legislation. But such efforts can quickly wear down a group unless there is some sort of focus. In order to build a viable movement, it was necessary to carve out a tangible and achievable goal.

One such target became public welfare—the income source upon which a large percentage of the community depended. Having built up a sense of trust and hope by directly responding to the urgent requests for help, the Neighborhood Center staff and their client allies were able to focus on action goals. There were false starts. A letter to the Welfare Commissioner requesting special grants for Christmas brought no response. But a demonstration to demand clothing yielded supplementary aid on the spot. There are risks in such efforts. Doling out such staples as food and clothing can be a way of placating the poor without really responding to them. And especially if some get and others do not, the protesters can be sidetracked to internecine warfare, leaving the welfare system untouched.

Instead, the organizers turned the modest initial victory to their own advantage. The immediate clothing allowances helped to establish their credibility in the eyes of their constituents, and it gave them hope of doing more. And those who received the grants stayed around to show their solidarity with those still waiting.[6]

The Neighborhood Services Center joined forces with a citywide movement of welfare recipients and, eventually, the National Welfare Rights Organization. In the end they obtained thousands of dollars in added benefits for welfare recipients. But more than that was achieved, for everyone had gained some self-respect and a feeling that he had the ability to work cooperatively with others. But, somehow, these fine aims elude the grasp of most professionals. With all their expertise, they miss a basic truth: that people and their problems do not exist in a vacuum. When the school social worker tries to help bolster the ego of a blighted youngster and then sends him back into the repressive, degrading brutality of the classroom, all his fine efforts are quickly wiped out. The family counselor who tries to enhance the image of a father in the eyes of his wife and children is no match for an economic system that shouts that the man is a surplus commodity without a useful role in society.

The Lincoln Hospital Neighborhood Service Center program succeeded in reaching and helping people because it made the connection between human problems at the retail and wholesale levels. It neither lost sight of people's need for a quick response to personal emergencies, nor did it become so myopic that it ignored the wider implications of the human misery it encountered.

One of the strengths of both the Long Beach Free Clinic and the Lincoln Hospital Neighborhood Service Center program was their refusal to be hemmed in by the boundaries of professional specialization. But there are specialized services, notably in the field of health care and legal services, which have been able to breach the social distance barriers between helper and client. One of these is California Rural Legal Assistance. One of its ventures has been its Senior Citizens' Project, which combines the talents of those in the social work and legal professions with those of nonprofessional older persons. Rather than offer a broad range of services on a walk-in basis, it has carved out advocacy of senior citizens' rights as its special concern.

Elderly individuals deprived of welfare benefits through bureaucratic callousness or simple carelessness, or those caught up in the indignity and fragmentation of health care services, have brought their grievances to the CRLA office. Most of the staff work of sorting out the issues and seeking redress from the system has been handled by older persons trained by the social worker in charge of the program. He and his lay advocates have handled all aspects of pressing their clients' claims, except those involving court litigation.[7]

CRLA has been in the wholesale as well as the retail end of helping. It has forced policy changes and reinterpretations amounting to millions of dollars in client benefits.

Each of these projects has had a limited life expectancy. By walking a tightrope it is possible for some innovative and change-oriented programs to outlive others, but eventually all go under or else go Establishment. Many of the early social settlement reformers managed to survive because they had independent incomes. But it seems clear that in the coming years, as in the past, most social workers will be employees of large service organizations. More of them will also go through some kind of professionalization process. Does this mean that they will reflect the worst and not the best traditions in social work? This does not have to happen. The lessons learned in the 1960's do not have to be lost. In fact, they *cannot* be if social work is to retain any of its viability as a profession.

What is a viable professionalism? To know this we must start not with the social worker but with the person he seeks to help. Over the years, social workers have touted the inherent dignity and worth of their clients and espoused a belief in client self-determination—all the while behaving as if their clients were weak and incapable of determining much of anything. The new professionalism is based upon a literal translation of the social work rhetoric into an operating set of assumptions.

The poor and alienated *are* persons of dignity, and they have the capacity to make choices in their own behalf. Their plight is much more a function of environmental pressures than of their own inadequacies. One can thus view the client as a rights-bearing individual, and the primary role of the social worker as aiding him in claiming his rights. Inhabitants of the inner city have the right to define their own destiny. The social worker is accountable to them first and foremost. Even though his salary comes from a system that is not subject to the client's direct control, the new breed of social worker places his obligation to the client ahead of his obligation to the welfare system.

This view of the poor is not something contrived; as

one frees himself from long-inbred assumptions about poor people, he is able to see them as real people who experience the full range of human emotions and occasionally exhibit remarkable energy and skill in coping with fantastic daily adversity.

One dimension of the new professionalism is the ability to transcend that social-distance barrier that now separates the social worker from those he aspires to serve. The workers in the Long Beach Free Clinic and in the Lincoln Hospital storefront centers were able to develop a spirit of closeness that broke down their clients' suspicion and sense of alienation. They could do this because they were genuinely allied with these victims in their quest for justice and self-fulfillment. When the pressure came from above, they demonstrated their real affection for their clients by not ducking behind the bureaucratic wall—as is so characteristic of other social workers.

The bridging of the social-distance barrier is not a one-sided process. For years low-income and minority group clients, sensing that they could not trust the social worker, drew a curtain around themselves. Since outright sullenness brought a nasty reaction from the worker, whereas wheedling deference passed for a successful relationship, most clients learned to say what the worker wanted to hear. But as militancy and self-awareness have grown among blacks and other minorities, the hostility that was always there has become more open. This is a shattering experience for the Harriet Norths, who had convinced themselves that they were "reaching" their clients.

At first glance, it may seem contradictory to speak of professionalism and closeness in the same breath. We are used to thinking of most professional disciplines as detached and analytic—never warm and spontaneous. But social workers have always sought to emphasize warmth and spontaneity, even while avoiding "over-identification." The aspiration is worthwhile, even if in practice social workers *have* often come off as cold and ungiving. Social work has faced a *double* barrier: one part is the natural tendency of professionalization to increase social distance, the other stems from the fact that social workers are employed in bureaucracies and are thus susceptible to all of the worst tendencies of bureaucrats.

This points to a key dimension of the new professionalism: *de*bureaucratization. In other words, social workers must be helped to resist and undermine the elements in their work situation that separate them from their clients. Their training must be directed specifically to helping them unfreeze and risk becoming over-identified, since for so long their clients have seen them as *under*identified.

Beyond the level of personal interaction, however, blacks, chicanos, and other minorities have a new sense of autonomy, a need to work out their own problems. But while these minorities now exemplify the sermon about "self-determination" preached over the years by social workers, these same social workers find the new relationship an uncomfortable one. How can social workers lower the social-distance barrier when client groups seem to be raising it? By understanding that the issue is not a matter of personal intimacy. Social workers, like all other middle-class liberals, have wanted to have pleasant personal relationships while actively or passively supporting institutional racism. Free clinics and neighborhood action groups have succeeded in bridging the gulf where traditional social work has failed, because bridging the gulf, in its superficial sense, has ceased to be their real object. The person who has already crossed over the social-distance barrier is not the one who gets angry when told to let poor people work things out for themselves, because he is more concerned with the realization of their aspirations than with winning their approval.

A second dimension of the new professionalism is shrewd pragmatism unencumbered by irrelevant norms of proper behavior. Because shrewdness by itself is neutral, it is a quality that can be employed by any master. So it cannot be allowed to become an end in itself. Social workers' best moments have come when they have been able to focus clearly on their real target. But too often they have turned their attention to matters of style.

As a result, social workers fret more about the way their colleagues present themselves in public than they do about the objectives of their activities. In one Eastern urban center, a city councilman transmitted to the local chapter of the National Association of Social Workers a critical report on the city's child welfare services. The report cited numerous instances of brutal and insensitive treatment of children and their parents, based mainly on the direct experiences of the staff members of the agency who had prepared the report. Many members of the social work group became incensed at the manner in which the councilman and the dissident staff members had presented the issue—meanwhile paying little attention to the substance of the report itself.

A community development project in Mississippi, financed by the Michael Schwerner Memorial Fund, came under criticism from local social workers because its director had bypassed them and otherwise disregarded professional decorum. The project's activities centered round aggressive attempts to get poor blacks onto the welfare rolls (no easy task in Mississippi) and get better representation of the poor on the board of the local antipoverty program. Again, the personal style of the director became more an issue than the fact that more "professional" elements in Mississippi had utterly failed to crack the tight control of the white power structure.[8]

But such diversionary preoccupations have not characterized the best passages in social work's history. More authentic antecedents of the new professionals can be found in such figures from social work's history as Dorothea Linde Dix and Harry L. Hopkins. Long before there was a social work profession, Miss Dix—acting anything but demure and diplomatic—badgered some thirty state legislatures into building facilities to care for the mentally ill. The notion of state mental hospitals sounds retrogressive today, but in the 1840's they were a great improvement over the unheated prisons and jails in which mental patients were housed like so many cattle.[9]

Political scientists remember Harry Hopkins as the wily henchman of President Franklin D. Roosevelt. During the Depression of the 1930's, Hopkins, who had once been a social worker, cut through red tape and got money moving into the hands of the poor while others cast about for explanations of poverty. Hopkins' shrill style and colorful language bore little resemblance to the "professional relationship" that has become the hallmark of the good caseworker.[10]

In the heady atmosphere of the 1960's, some social workers became entranced with the style of direct confrontation. When this became a way to gratify their own desire for excitement instead of a tool to be used selectively, it was just as irrelevant as the criticism by colleagues who viewed *any* conflict as unprofessional.

The pragmatic orientation is an important foundation for action, for it helps social workers to separate the relevant from the irrelevant and focus on their objectives. But pragmatism is *not* a set of skills. More than ever in the past, today's social worker needs a wide array of tools if he is to be effective. In giving up the protective cloak of narrow specialization, social workers must respond to widely diverse situations.

Take, for example, the staff of the Long Beach Free Clinic. The young people who went there needed help then and there—this one with a drug problem and that one with an induction notice. The staff would have quickly lost the trust of the street people had they sent them off to be on some other agency's waiting list.

One of the image problems social workers have always had is the fact that it all looks so easy. Talk to a person about his problems? Give advice—advice that often comes in the form of interminable questions without answers? Everybody from the cop on the corner to the next-door neighbor gives advice about personal problems. This has led many persons to question the need for social workers at all. Why strain at getting them over their professional myopia when poor people are really their own best advocates? Social workers—who needs them? The professionals' low batting average in exacting concessions from the system in behalf of society's victims has not helped to alter this perception.

Poor people do have a central role to play on their own behalf. But notwithstanding the exciting potentialities of poor people united, there is more need than ever before for an intermediary cadre if there are to be lasting gains. If there is one lesson to be learned from the turmoil of recent years, it is that the Establishment has the resources to outmaneuver and outwait poor people who are operating on their own. The welfare industry keeps becoming more complex, more remote from the suffering in the streets. It is harder for poor people to locate the targets for their protest. Under these circumstances, a professional group that can carry the message inside the system, locate the weak spots in the castle wall, and use the system's resources against itself, becomes especially strategic. Given a different brand of professionalism, the social worker can run interference for the client—reach a key decision-maker while the client gets put off at the reception desk. Chapter VII will trace the many strategic points within and around the welfare establishment where social workers are located. They can begin to put their potential influence to work if they can be schooled in the proper orientation with the necessary tools to do the job.

And there are the kinds of strategic knowledge that the social worker—once his professional education is focused in the right direction—can acquire as a matter of course. The poor know very well where it hurts, and they can tell it much better than the social worker. But they do not necessarily know what else has been tried in other places and other times. Then there are those dull but crucial bits of information about congressional appropriations and cash transfers, mostly written in bureaucratic jargon well calculated to befuddle the layman. The citizen who tells the chairman of a legislative committee that he is irrelevant will probably earn some headlines and little more. Meanwhile, the decision the chairman makes may affect the destinies of thousands of children and their families. It helps to have somebody around who has better facts than the chairman, who has his ear, and who knows how important the chairman actually is to the fate of the bill in question.

But of all the expertise that the new professional needs, none is more important than the ability to deal with his own agency. This spells the difference between the Harry Hopkinses and the Harriet Norths. In view of the vital relationship between social work and the social welfare industry, it is a crucial difference.

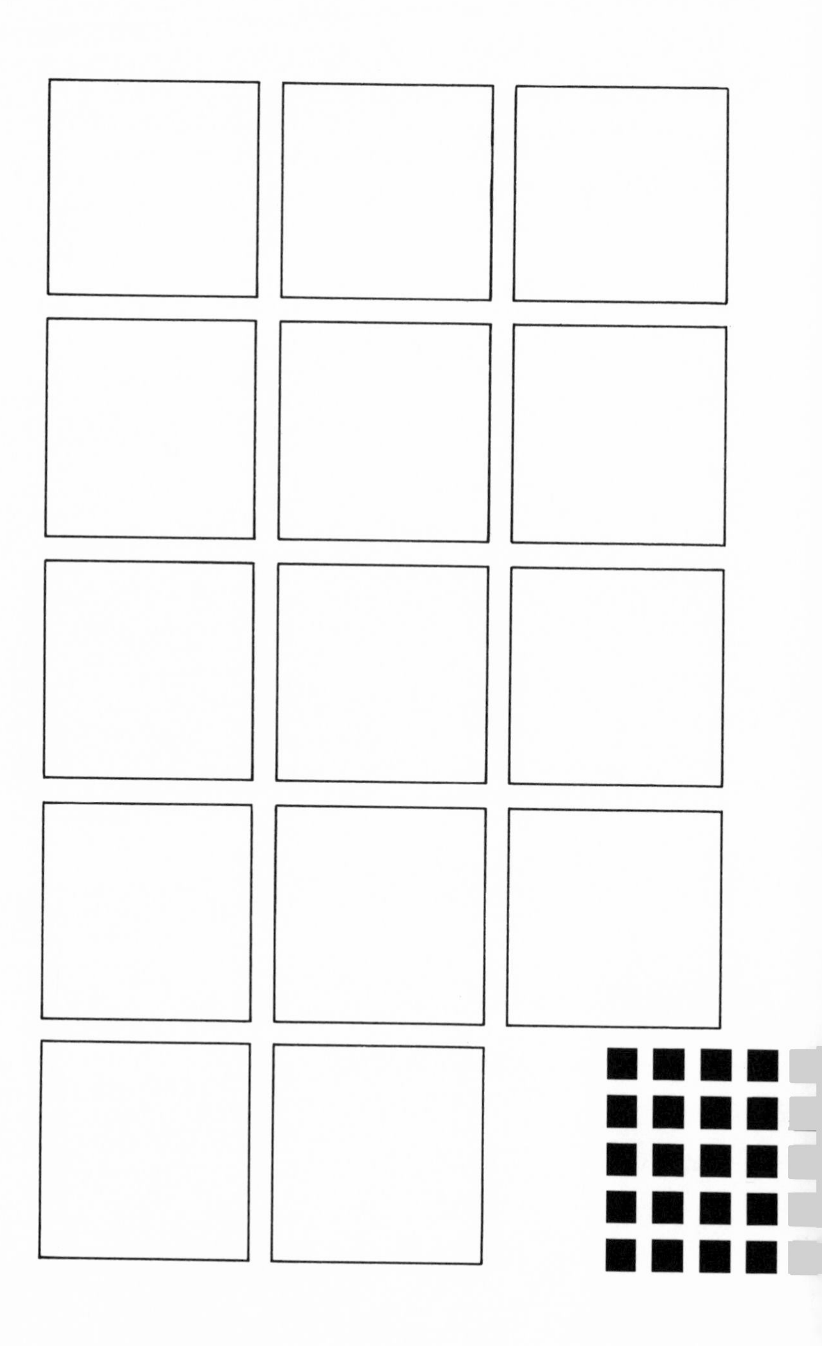

CHAPTER 7
A PROFESSION OF BUREAUCRATS

To understand the social work profession and its present predicament, one must come to grips with the central role that social service bureaucracies have played in social work since its inception. Why have social workers nursed the idealized image of themselves as champions of the underdogs, all the while actually protecting entrenched interests against the underdogs? One overriding reason is the fact that social workers have rarely been their own masters. Although they do not like to admit it, they are essentially glorified bureaucrats. A significant minority are private practitioners, but social work is clearly an *employee* profession. This fact helps to explain a deep-seated and pervasive compliance mentality in social workers.

A number of years ago, a psychologist named Stanley Milgram carried out exhaustive studies of obedience to authority. His subjects were required to administer shocks to strangers; they believed they were assisting him in an experimental study of the effects of pain on memory. In actuality Milgram was studying their own response to commands. He had anticipated that his subjects would resist his order to push the voltage to the points marked EXTREME SHOCK and DANGER: SEVERE SHOCK. He was wrong. Most of them went doggedly on simply because that was the requested behavior.

Milgram found that even when the "victim" pounded on the wall and then fell ominously silent or screamed out asking for mercy, more than three out of five of his subjects kept turning up the voltage indicator. After testing more than a thousand persons in this way, Milgram concluded:

> With numbing regularity good people were seen to knuckle under the demands of authority and perform actions that were callous and severe. . . . A

> substantial proportion of people do what they are told to do, irrespective of the content of the act and without limitations of conscience, so long as they perceive that the command comes from legitimate authority.[1]

If Milgram's subjects yielded that readily to someone who had no real authority over them, we can begin to understand what happens to social workers whose livelihood and careers depend on following orders. This helps explain why all but three members of the Alameda County Welfare Department's staff went along with the night raids. And why the Harriet Norths believe they are doing good. And if some aspects of her work trouble Harriet, she calls upon a finely developed set of professional rationalizations to justify her behavior to herself.

Benny Parrish and Bill Berkan had to fight their organizations in order to maintain their integrity, and when Harriet North capitulated it was her agency that exacted the price from her. So social welfare institutions are a strategic link between social workers and the society at large.

Social work initially became professional because social service bureaucracies needed a better grade of personnel. The first schools of social work were started by agencies—not universities—around the turn of the century. Even today, the agencies dominate the education of most social work students. There is a strong tradition of apprentice-like training in the field as the core of graduate social work education. In most schools this still means that students spend more than half of their time in social agencies, the majority being taught by agency employees to meet agency expectations. Only in recent years have schools begun to break away from this agency-centered pattern.

It is little wonder, then, that the principle lingers on that the social worker's first loyalty should be to his employer! Empirical studies have confirmed that this is, in fact, the primary identification of most social workers, regardless of whether they work in agencies that are themselves identified with social work values or antagonistic to them.[2]

In part, the coldness and hostility of many social workers toward clients stem from the fact that their agencies are essentially anti-client to begin with. Perhaps the more troubling this is for the worker at the outset, the more he turns against the client—an unhappy resolution of his dilemma. But social workers do not react in isolation to the conflicting demands on them. Staff members interact constantly, sharing their frustrations and developing a common culture. This peer culture in fact becomes a stronger influence on the individual worker than the formal expectations of the agency hierarchy. That is why it is so hard for a worker to free himself of agency biases once they become instilled in him. The social work profession can offer another set of expectations to offset agency attitudes, but in the past it has failed to do so.

In giving their basic allegiance to the agency rather than to people in need, social workers have accurately perceived what their professional community desires. It is only recently that the National Association of Social Workers (NASW) has begun to challenge this order of priority. A few years ago, NASW served a very different function. In November, 1959, a young woman known in association annals only as "Mrs. B" went to work as the executive director of a new organization engaged in planning in the fields of health, welfare, and recreation. A year later she was fired, ostensibly on grounds of incompetence. Mrs. B claimed that the dismissal was based upon her membership—as a private citizen—in a group working for racial integration. As a member of NASW, she filed a complaint under provisions designed to protect members' rights to engage in social and political action. Mrs. B's petition was rejected. The official version of the incident speaks for itself:

> Mrs. B. was obligated to choose between resigning from her position and resigning from the antisegregation organization when it became apparent that the discharge of her civic responsibility made it impossible for her to discharge her professional obligations in the particular post she held. The ethical pledge of social workers states: "I regard as my primary obligation the welfare of the individual or group served which includes action for improving social conditions." The group served in this instance was the board of the planning council employing Mrs. B, which itself existed for the purpose of improving social conditions.[3]

But object lessons, such as the case of Mrs. B, are of little use if they are not publicized. The story of the incident appeared under the headline, "Agency Exonerated by Commission on Complaint Filed by Member," as the only news item on page 1 of the November, 1962, issue of *Personnel Information*—at that time NASW's organ for listing job openings. What better place to post warnings against anti-agency attitudes? The message was carried to the students of one school of social work by a key staff member of NASW; he had been invited to speak at one of their programs, and he chose to report on the case of Mrs. B. It is doubtful that its significance was lost on his audience.

But by the end of the 1960's, the National Association of Social Workers was beginning to look increasingly less like an apologist for organized social welfare. In striking contrast to the tone of the case involving Mrs. B, an official statement in 1969 declared that the social worker's obligation to his client's welfare took precedence over his obligation to his employer; where the two sets of interest were in conflict, the worker's first loyalty was to the client.[4] In 1971, the association sought for the first time to move directly into the business of policing agency practices in behalf of the rights of clients and potential clients. And just as the case of Mrs. B had been widely publicized by NASW within the professional community, the association now made it a point to publicize a number of decisions in which the social worker—not his employer—was the winner.

Ethical codes and other regulatory mechanisms have traditionally served to protect entrenched interests—in social work as in other professions. But the social workers have begun to use this potentially powerful machinery toward a different end: to pressure the field into living up to its high purpose.

What this suggests is a key role for the organized professional community as a countervailing force against the entrenched power of vast service bureaucracies. This is essential if individual social workers are to see themselves as agents of social change. They must feel the full weight of their profession behind them or they will be picked off easily, one by one.

For both the individual worker and the professional community at large, one of the most crippling constraints is the conviction that they are puny in the face of a huge and unyielding monolith. Having come to terms with the basic amorality and dehumanization of the system and the way in which they have been used by it, social workers are inclined to feel defeated when they contemplate the possibility of ever influencing its course. Such cynicism would serve exactly the same function as the old complicity: namely, to discourage efforts to change things. Thus, the self-fulfilling prophecy: the pessimism would induce behavior that would prove that the pessimism was right.

But the cynics pride themselves on being realistic, so let us be realistic. The social welfare industry is neither monolithic nor infinitely powerful. Take the most powerful single force in the welfare field, the United States Government. Our mind conjures up a vast juggernaut impervious to all attempts to alter its course. The reality is a number of identifiable points where decisions actually get made. The people making the decisions are human beings, susceptible to all those influences to which other human beings are subject. Some observers have commented that official Washington is like nothing so much as an overgrown small town, with all its typical petty bickering. The difference, of course, lies in the monumental consequences of Washington's pettiness for the rest of us.

The points where crucial decisions in the welfare field get made can be enumerated. They tend to be made by single individuals—located within the administration or the congressional establishment. We think of the members of Congress as wielding great power —as indeed they do. But most of them have to vote on issues about which they have the scantiest of information, with the result that they are highly dependent upon other people who don't vote but who do have expertise on specific issues. Few persons are expert on more than a narrow range of information; this makes many persons dependent on many other persons. Ranged throughout bureaus in the Department of Health, Education, and Welfare are the people who often determine how issues are defined and the sorts of choices the members of Congress can make. Another key point is in congressional committees; they have experts on their staffs, but experts with varying amounts of expertise. Much of the actual decision-making goes on between committee counsels and administration aides. Outside of committee chairmen, most members of Congress carve out specific areas in which they become conversant with the issues. It so happens that welfare is a subject on which few bother to become expert because it is not a particularly popular subject—with congressmen or their constituents. All of which makes those experts in the Department of Health, Education, and Welfare highly strategic.

Social workers fill many such positions in the Department of Health, Education, and Welfare. Insofar as this work becomes a career for them, they tend to orient their work to the organization of which they are part—just as the social worker in a local agency becomes identified with his organization. Their professional community makes few if any demands on them to be different, which is probably a reflection of the insecurity of social workers as a group. As one gets to know the social workers in the federal establishment, one finds individuals who are on the whole more dedicated to human betterment than the average, but whose sensitivity to social change varies greatly. And above all they have learned to be good team players.

When social workers complain about the federal establishment and its insensitivity to human needs, they are complaining in part about those colleagues on the inside. The professional community must learn how to make demands on these social workers—demands great enough to have some impact on the course of welfare policies. This may be a more vital route for social workers to travel in bringing about social change than sending delegations to meet with congressmen and senators.

The social welfare industry is not a monolith. Much of the action, both governmental and voluntary, takes place outside Washington—for instance, in the ten regional offices of the federal government scattered around the country. More and more, decisions about program-funding and maintenance of decent standards of service are made in the regional offices, in line with the current philosophy of decentralization. Again, the regional structure is not something vast and inscrutable, but real people in ten key cities: Boston, New York, Philadelphia, Atlanta, Chicago, Dallas, Kansas City, Denver, San Francisco, and Seattle. Within a specific area of responsibility—such as state compliance with federal rules on civil rights or requirements in a particular set of programs—the regional staff may be very small; it may, in fact, be a single person. A social worker? Frequently, yes. Ten regions—and ten key persons within a specific area of policy—for the whole country.

One of the least appreciated levels of government is the state. State legislators generally are not known to their constituents—which is much less true of congressmen or city councilmen. One reason for this is that congressmen and councilmen are persons one approaches with a personal request or a complaint about service. Meanwhile, most federal programs are actually designed and implemented at the state level. Over the years, the federal government has passed many laws calling for social services or direct money payments. But most of these are based on grants-in-aid—federal payment to the states, which must put up part of the cash and actually write the program. True, these state programs must comply with federal guidelines, but within that limitation they can vary tremendously in scope, adequacy of benefits, etc. The advent of revenue sharing—under which the federal government channels block grants, with few strings attached, to the states—is increasing state and local variability.

More than at both the federal and local levels, professional social workers have been running state social welfare programs. In recent years a number of states have been eliminating long-standing requirements for social work education in a number of such jobs, but the state machinery in many programs is still dominated by social workers. What is true of congressmen is even truer of state legislators. Most lack any staff at all, and what staff they do have is generally preoccupied with the chronic task of getting the boss reelected. Legislative leaders and state party organizations—the two standard guides for the individual legislator—have little interest in welfare in general and can't understand what social services are all about. But social workers at the state level—who potentially have a more strategic role than those at the federal level—have been least inclined to use their position to bring about social change. And what about the demands from the professional community? The National Association of Social Workers is *least* well organized at the state level, least able to bring any kind of leverage to bear on anybody for anything. Courses in schools of social work, insofar as they deal with social policy, tend to ignore state government for the more glamorous issues at the national level.

The social welfare industry is not a monolith. And social workers are located throughout the system, in places where they *can* begin to reshape it, if their professional training prepares them to do it and their professional colleagues demand it. There are a finite number of key positions in the nation's capital, ten regional offices, fifty state capitals. And then there are city and county agencies and a wide range of voluntary organizations at the local level. And to start a revolution in the social welfare industry it is not necessary to focus on every locality.

Crammed together in the ghettos of ten large cities

are over 6,000,000 blacks, two out of every seven blacks in the country as a whole. To transform the systems of human services in these cities alone would make a major impact on the lives of blacks in the United States and pave the way for a basic revolution in the social welfare industry. We are talking about ten welfare departments, with the power to bring about basic changes without altering *one* word in existing welfare legislation.

In most of these cities, a small handful of major hospitals handle the bulk of health care delivery to the poor. During the day health is parceled out in the outpatient department, while at night the emergency room takes over. These places are used to give experience to interns and residents, most of whom find poor and minority people offensive. And they are free to show it, because the institution and the society that has established it make very clear that health is a privilege to be reserved for those who can pay.

The atmosphere is intimidating and oppressive. If Mr. García goes to the hospital instead of the welfare department, the script changes slightly, but he is greeted by the same air of suspicion, the same assaults on his personal dignity. He wants medication? (Is he on drugs?) Backache? (Probably faking so he can get on welfare.) And he soon discovers that he is not a person who is suffering but rather a machine to be put through an impersonal assembly line called medical care. One university professor who went to the outpatient department of his university's hospital was completely unnerved by the badgering to which he was subjected until the hospital staff discovered that he was not a charity case.

But what if outpatient clinics and emergency rooms in these hospitals, instead of dehumanizing and destroying the people they are supposed to serve, were to become life-giving and dignity-enhancing? All of these hospitals have social service departments. Suppose the social workers in those departments applied literally the high purpose spelled out in the social work profession's liturgy. If they did they would not tolerate the conditions that prevail in their institutions—at least not without a good fight.

Ten cities, ten public school systems, most of them employing social workers. Suppose these social workers seriously asked themselves how they were serving the avowed priorities of the National Association of Social Workers—to fight racism and poverty—and whether they were fulfilling the expectation that social workers will act as advocates for their clients.

The private sector of social welfare in each of these ten cities is dominated by a handful of fund-raising and service organizations. In some cases, a single oligarchy controls the destinies of voluntary social agencies in the community. While the business community controls the financial resources that flow into these agencies, businessmen have little understanding of the workings of the social welfare industry and are highly dependent upon the welfare professionals who run the operations. And in each of these cities is a chapter of the National Association of Social Workers. These chapters have the potential power to enforce upon their professional brethren in strategic agency positions the obligation to behave professionally.

These are all highly strategic vantage points where social workers can make a basic impact on social welfare and, ultimately, on the quality of life in the United States. But they only begin to scratch the surface. The truth is that social welfare is literally crawling with social workers, located throughout every part of the country. Obviously the social workers have not been able to translate their strategic positions into a different kind of social welfare system.

The social welfare industry is neither monolithic nor infinitely powerful. The points of major impact on the system are definable, and the persons making the major decisions can be identified. And many of them are social workers. It is no longer possible for the social work profession to hide behind the claim that the real decisions are being made elsewhere. Rather, the issue is whether social work can arm itself with the resolve and the expertise to begin making a different kind of decision.

The intent is not to sound glib. The reader of this book may not be in one of the strategic positions in the federal or state establishment, or in one of those local public or voluntary agencies. What can a single social worker do now?

At the end of this book, we suggest some ways in which to challenge the status quo in the social service system. It is not intended as a complete course of study. It is a way of making a start. If this were all there was to it, we could reduce the whole social work arsenal to a do-it-yourself manual and be done with all the professional paraphernalia. But clearly this is not all there is to it. Over the years social scientists have made exhaustive inquiries into the workings of bureaucratic organization, including social welfare agencies. Thus social workers have at hand a vast lore on what makes service systems function as they do, and on the service functionaries within them.

Social work schools are beginning to devote more time to teaching their students this content. But rarely have social work educators approached this subject from the standpoint of the institutional subversive. And it is basically as an institutional subversive that the new social work professional must now enter the welfare system. He will not necessarily intend to completely overturn the organization—although doubtless there are some that can only be salvaged by being destroyed. More typically the new professional will make selective use of his skill to bring about basic institutional reform.

CHAPTER 8
A MORE RELEVANT EDUCATION FOR SOCIAL WORK

Social workers in the field are vaguely aware that something fundamental is happening to social work education. Professionals—who only a few years ago were taught the "time-tested truths" about psychosocial development—are bewildered by a new language of social science terms and a new readiness of students (students unafraid of being labeled "resistive") to question. Particularly in some of the newer schools, unshackled by a long tradition and an entrenched clique of senior faculty, there are revolutionary changes going on. Social work practitioners either learn about these changes from yeasty new workers fresh out of school or they struggle to cope with a new brand of student coming into their agencies to do field work. The older social workers find it all very disturbing and are sure that the current crop of students is not learning practice skills (the skills *they* learned as students, that is). They may accuse the faculty of fomenting the revolution, but within the schools themselves the faculty are often running just to keep up with their students.

The educational revolution still has a long way to go. Many of the largest and most prestigious schools of social work have been able to ward off change in their key curriculum areas. But social work education is going through changes—as it well needs to. The revolution is already going on.

If social work has been the unloved profession, its educational enterprise has been at least as unadmired in the academic community. In part, this attitude reflects rank campus snobbery, related to the social worker's historic involvement in the grubby issues of poverty and community disorganization. But it also stems from an accurate perception of the intellectual hollowness that has characterized social work education until very recently.

Social workers, generally insecure about the acceptance of their field as a profession, grasped at the forms of academic respectability without its content. Hence, the two-year master's degree was the entry threshold until recently. Within the graduate curriculum, the master's thesis became an additional symbol of respectability. Each student was required to complete such a project, but this was a far cry from the rigorous scholarship to which they pretended. A common practice of the casework student, for instance, was to write an analysis of several cases tied loosely together by a common theme. In one school, the thesis included a description of the student's own educational conversion—a kind of parting confession.

The obvious intellectual bankruptcy in all this has led some observers directly to the radical conclusion voiced in an earlier part of this book: is not the whole involvement with universities and their academic rat race a huge mistake for social work? Would it not be wiser just to send aspiring social workers out to *work* in free clinics and neighborhood action centers? This brings us back to the relationship between professionalism and its base of expertise.

We might revisit those social workers doing curbstone therapy in Long Beach, California. They are drawing upon professional skill—not just their love of humanity and their hatred of the Vietnam war. The fact that the worker is draped over a parked car may make him seem like the next door neighbor draped over the back fence giving advice to her friend, but in reality that social worker has to hear things that would go right past the friendly neighbor. And he has to know when *not* to give advice. It is not that the social worker's judgment is perfect; out of their insecurity social workers have sometimes tried to claim that—with a low batting average for results. But the worker has more to draw upon in the way of *other* people's experience accumulated over the years—some of it tested out systematically.

One of the functions of the social worker, in fact, is to help the layman learn what is useful in social work knowledge and practice skills. The grass roots leader will always have special access to his people that the professional will not. And rather than try to be all things to all people—a kind of instant Batman—the social worker needs to expand the natural skills of people in the community without distorting them. One of the hopeful developments in social work education in recent years has been a growing interest in working with lay persons who, in turn, work with their own people. Especially as the social work job market has contracted, this promising thrust has had to fight off the old tendency toward monopoly.

The solution to social work educational weaknesses is not to scrap social work education but to change it into something more vital. All revolutions carry in them a tendency toward overkill, a readiness to reduce the old order to symbols and then to set out and destroy all the symbols. It is tempting to think of eliminating the whole enterprise. But what would this yield? A new wave of free clinics and community action programs? No. It would produce an army of bureaucrats completely subject to the dictates of the social welfare industry. Most social workers will be employed in welfare bureaucracies. A viable professional education provides one of the few means of giving them an alternate view of themselves and the possibilities for social work.

Thus, the reaction to academic pretentiousness in social work has led to a basic questioning of all academic content—precisely at a time when social work has urgently needed rapid development of its scientific foundations in order to cope with the scientific explosion in the social welfare industry.

Social work professionals do, in fact, need intellectual hardware—they need it very badly if they are to offer anything beyond good intentions and a sensitive soul. Important though those attributes are, they are hardly a match for the forces with which social work must deal in the years ahead. And in order to make knowledge work for them—instead of controlling them—the social workers must learn to make discriminating use of it and be able to translate it into guides for action. Social work has been at its best in the past when it has drawn from a wide range of fields. One of the more hopeful signs in recent decades has been the readiness to look to many fields in the social and behavioral sciences, instead of allowing psychoanalytic psychology to remain *the* central core of social work knowledge.

The scientific revolution sweeping social work education is not its first. In the second and third decades of this century, Freudian theory rapidly became the intellectual core for social work's practice theory. More than this, it became an enveloping and stultifying mystique that discouraged critical evaluation of its basic assumptions. The profession was especially susceptible to this kind of theological non-science because of its historic paucity of theory and systematic research. There was also the need for a feeling of certainty in a field that tampered with human lives.

When social scientists began invading social work faculties in the late 1950's and early 1960's, the turmoil they unleashed was predictable. Established senior faculty members suddenly found the ground underneath them shifting. No longer could they use clinical "insight" to intimidate their critics. In all, the revolution was a liberating experience. It forced social workers to question old shibboleths as never before. The student who asked questions or—heaven forbid—knew more about a subject than his professor, could not be psyched out. The tables were turned, and now it was the old guard instead of the new breed who were on the defensive.

And what is the substance of the change—other than a more inquiring and critical spirit? Not that the importance of the change in spirit should be minimized. That in itself can prevent the enshrinement of a new orthodoxy, built around "new" theories that soon come to look very old. In other words, the scientific revolution must be a continuous revolution. But there is also new substance.

With few exceptions, social work schools built virtually their entire curricula around the Freudian mystique; the exceptions had even more orthodox outlooks. The Freudian approach was not only a theoretical system (a system, incidentally, which few social work students ever studied in the original), it was also a way of thinking—about clients, about colleagues, about oneself. Now a major target of the scientific revolution has been this Freudian core—its lack of empirical validation, its lack of scientific skepticism, and its pomposity. In the traditional regimen, students in some social work schools spent more classroom hours studying this cult than studying practice techniques per se. But it mattered little, because the benchmark of all wisdom in the classroom and the field was the same cult. Today fewer and fewer schools operate under this stultifying and redundant system. In most of the courses in human behavior and social environment the schools draw upon a range of theoretical approaches cutting across several scientific disciplines. The Freudian wisdom may still be there, but it is no longer the central theme. True, casework teachers may act as if nothing had changed, but now they are more likely to be challenged by their students—who may well cite contrary material they have acquired in other classes.

There has been rapidly growing interest in service agencies as institutions. The new content in social systems theory and organizational analysis has matched the increased awareness of the importance of the agency environment in influencing social workers' professional behavior. New social work graduates emerge from school, not only with an acute concern about their relationship to the employing agency, but also with a far greater degree of sophistication about the workings of the agency.

One mushrooming area of social work education content at times borders on the faddish: that dealing with social class and ethnic differences. Some students have trouble distinguishing between intellectual content and political fervor—an inevitable consequence of the heated atmosphere in which such offerings have been adopted. But in the long run these courses will be an important corrective to middle-class bias and naïveté.

At the present time, material from the fields of political science and economics has made little headway in many schools—in others it seems to be unrelated to the bread-and-butter practice content. In part this may arise from a realistic perception of the social worker's role: he seldom has access to the levers for fundamental political and economic decision-making until long after he has left his social work training. At the same time, content on social welfare policy has become increasingly bread-and-butter. Traditionally, this content consisted of dreary recitations of history. Today, it is more likely to focus on techniques of social problem analysis and policy development and evaluation, necessary tools for the would-be change-agent.

The scientific revolution has helped to dislodge the mystique surrounding the master's degree itself. Social work education is increasingly viewed as a continuum—stretching from technical training at the junior college level all the way to doctoral study. In part this came in response to increasing empirical evidence that the graduate of the two-year master's degree program was not all that easy to distinguish from persons with other combinations of training and experience. One interpretation of this evidence is that social work education, therefore, is unnecessary. But in the light of the increasing complexity of the social institutions and social problems with which social workers must deal, the more realistic appraisal is that social work education needs to develop even more sophisticated tools.

Science is neutral, but its effects are not. Its potential promise and hazard for social work are illustrated by one of the new thrusts in the profession: behavioral modification. This systematic approach to changing client functioning is built on a solid base of rigorous experimentation. Its effectiveness in removing troublesome behavioral symptoms has been experimentally demonstrated. It can therefore claim a scientific legitimacy that psychoanalytic psychology never could. Clearly, here is a powerful tool that the social worker can use to intervene in human problems. But its very potency creates certain risks.

Like earlier approaches, behavioral modification tends to focus the worker's attention on the person experiencing the problems—and implicitly to treat this person as the locus of the difficulty. Thus, Johnny's conflict with school is Johnny's problem, to be solved inside Johnny. Social workers can then put on a new and more efficient set of blinders that lead them away from questioning what the teacher is doing to Johnny and his classmates, or how the slum environment impinges on the entire educational process.

But the potentially more insidious side of behavioral modification is its effectiveness as an instrument of people-control. While enthusiasts proffer such safeguards as contracts with the client and voluntary participation in treatment, the history of social work as a means of social control raises the possibility of a benign kind of brainwashing if great care is not used. Notwithstanding practices to the contrary, social work has held out as one of its central tenets the client's right to determine his own life and his freedom to make choices. As in the past, the new technology can undermine such principles in subtle ways.[1]

Likewise, new technologies of information storage and retrieval are attracting the interest of social work educators and administrators. As always there are all manner of reasons why the field "must" use these tools. And the people who employ them are not demons in the flesh, though the implications of their use overall may indeed be demonic.

When social work leaders evolved the principle of confidentiality, the cornerstone of the client's right to privacy, they were dealing with primitive techniques of information management that relied on human ability to remember and record. As long as social workers were bound to secrecy and agency files were kept under lock and key, it was possible to keep some control over the uses and misuses of information. But even then, facts about clients were ordinarily shared between agencies without clients' knowledge. This was enough of a problem when the information-sharing stayed mainly within one community. But new data retrieval technology makes it vastly more difficult to control such information once it is obtained. Various fail-safe systems for protecting client privacy have been suggested, but once data are gathered there is probably no foolproof way of protecting confidentiality. In the social services there is only one real protection for clients' privacy, and that is a social worker who understands the underlying issues involved and his own responsibility in relation to them. Again, the problem is for social work to control its technology, and not the other way around.[2]

The intellectual challenge posed by social work's rediscovery of the social sciences has had a cleansing if disturbing impact on the profession. The invasion of social work schools by sociologists, psychologists, and others has helped to break the intellectual stranglehold of Freud. One of the major discoveries for social workers has been the accumulation of evidence as to *why* social work was unloved—or at least unrespected. There are, for example, the aforementioned studies of worker behavior and attitudes, showing clearly that the social worker as bureaucrat took precedence over the social worker as professional. A rude shock for a field that sought so hard to make it into the ranks of the entrepreneurial professions!

But even more unsettling were studies that purported to show little if any difference between professionals and non-professionals in the social services.[3] These studies have been of widely varying quality, but they have raised fundamental questions about what social work education does teach. In justice to the profession, it must be pointed out that the kinds of things social workers attempt to do are extremely hard to measure. Some of the studies showing little impact for professionalism have also shown little impact for any kind of intervention. Rather than conclude that social workers need no special education, one needs to understand the much more profound lesson: interventions geared to altering human functioning without any regard to altering the environment within which that functioning goes on are doomed to failure. This is especially true in the case of the poor, whose tangible external adversity looms so large in their problems.

One important effect of the studies questioning the mystique of the master's degree was to give legitimacy to the expansion of professional education and professional status to include the baccalaureate level. It has become crystal clear that persons graduating from a well-rounded undergraduate social work program, including practice courses and field practice, can do a creditable job at carrying out many functions that master's degree graduates have done in the past. Currently there is a vast shake-up going on in the format as well as the content of social work education. Education for direct service positions in social agencies is shifting increasingly to the bachelor's level, while more and more master's degree students are preparing for supervisory and training and consulting functions that were once viewed as requiring years and years of experience. The standard two-year master's degree program is on its way to being replaced by a four-year social welfare concentration at the undergraduate level, and a fifth year in graduate school.

The problem that now faces social work educators is how to select the most relevant content and compress it into a shorter time span. The problem is complicated by the knowledge revolution going on in social work—a revolution that touched off a major crisis in schools of social work across the country when it began in the early 1960's. The social scientists who joined social work faculties and the growing crop of doctoral graduates precipitated a frantic overhaul of curricula. Often the changes were more apparent than real, since field practice in social agencies still held a central place in the minds of both students and faculty. But the intellectual revolution focused social work educators' attention more firmly than ever on academic credentials, albeit with more academic substance than before. In so doing it tended to move social work education even farther away from direct practical involvement in problems out in the community. As it affected faculty recruitment and student admissions, it also meant an even greater preponderance of middle-class whites.[4]

Initially, the revolts against intellectual mediocrity and against the welfare establishment tended to merge. The same young professors and students threw nasty questions at older faculty members inside the schools and at welfare and education officials outside. One reason for this was that the protest against injustice was dominated by campus types who had the loose schedules, the protection against retaliation, and the ability to draft eloquent exposés, press releases, and petitions. Eventually, the alliance between academician and insurgent broke down. The alliance was a victim of the rising outcry of students against an outworn and irrelevant intellectual tradition. And even more formidable was the changing nature of the urban ferment, particularly as it involved blacks and other minorities within and outside the university.

Student protest in schools of social work has been a pale imitation of the raging conflict that hit university campuses in the late 1960's. Characteristically, the social work students have issued carefully worded petitions, held orderly if not friendly negotiating sessions with administrators, and employed such direct weapons as strikes and boycotts only sparingly. A strain of reasonableness has marked such efforts, in contrast to some of the more violent confrontations in other departments. In one school of social work, militant students decided to decorate the premises with graffiti—slogans charging the faculty with irrelevance and the administration with dictatorship. It is noteworthy that they wrote their slogans on placards that they attached to the walls with tape that could readily be removed without leaving a mark (if nothing else, the social work student revolt is genteel).

But such mild disruptions have had an impact on social work education—largely because of the eagerness of teachers and administrators to respond. So student participation in decision-making has come with little resistance; often the faculty and not the students have been the ones to take the initiative, in order to avert even this kind of unpleasantness. And the Council of Social Work Education has included a significant student voice in school affairs as one of its expectations for social work schools.

Together, the intellectual revolution and the student unrest transformed the atmosphere of the social work educational process. Historically, social work students were essentially viewed as clients. Accordingly, the teacher was expected to make an educational diagnosis of the learner in order to prescribe the best experience to meet his needs. There were therapeutic overtones in all aspects of social work education.

So conceived, the educational process was well suited to training social work students to become obedient, cooperative, and introspective social agency employees later on. But now this clinical approach to the educational process is fast losing its legitimacy. Although the practice still goes on informally, it is no longer sanctioned. Having begun to emancipate students, social work educators cannot suddenly say they did not mean to. The effects of this beginning can be vast, for one of the props of professional subservience to organizational domination has been knocked away.

Yet in the long run, social work education's true impact on practice will depend upon the kind of mission it sees for itself. And a major force in defining that mission has been the entry into social work schools of increasing numbers of blacks and other minorities—groups that have been excluded in the past by social work's preoccupation with academic credentials, yet who perhaps have the most intimate understanding of the struggle for human decency.

The recruitment of black students and teachers began as a kind of numbers game, with the schools and the Council on Social Work Education devoting far more attention to percentages than to the effective preparation of the new recruits or their impact upon the field. The Council still seems preoccupied with percentages, but it is beginning to develop special aids for schools for making the enterprise a creative and productive one. Meanwhile, schools of social work that find themselves hemmed in by university-wide standards of student admission and faculty advancement, reflecting traditional academic norms, must fight alone.

The most tragic resolution of the problem would be for blacks and other minority group members simply to become absorbed into the traditional academic mold, giving up their linkage to the communities from which they come as a price for making it in the system. In other words, social work education needs what these new elements have to offer at least as much as the newcomers need social work education.

Out of seventy students entering the master's degree program in social work at the University of California at Los Angeles in 1967, there were five blacks and a small sprinkling of other minorities. This pattern of white dominance was typical of most social work schools across the country. Three years later at UCLA, the situation was dramatically reversed: three out of four entering students were blacks or from other minority backgrounds. The change was deliberate, the result of a confrontation between black and chicano students and the faculty and administration.[5]

Shifts in the composition of student bodies at other schools indicated that this was more than a token development. One school established a policy of admitting a majority of "Third World" students; another set a quota of 50-50 blacks and whites; others aimed for one-third black and other minorities. The emphasis on percentages disturbed many social work educators, to whom the concept of quotas was repugnant:

> a throwback to the numerous class restrictions of Czarist Russia; a painful reminder of American immigration policy which favored northern and western Europeans over those from the eastern and southern countries, and which practically excluded people from the countries of Asia.[6]

But what is happening touches off the more fundamental fear among some liberals that educational values are being sacrificed in behalf of political appeasement. The most common comparison drawn is with Nazi Germany. No matter that for years the same liberals worried little or not at all that institutional racism virtually excluded minority group members from the academic credentialing system. But the concerns need to be viewed on their merits.

Is the large-scale movement of ethnic minorities into social work faculties and student bodies purely a political takeover that will leave professionalism in a shambles? On the contrary, it can help to breathe an important kind of vigor and relevance into the educational enterprise. We can look at this on two levels: the experience of the individual learner and the quality of the educating process itself.

The trickle of black students into schools of social

work in the past has meant that the minority have been in what is to all intents and purposes a white institution. Admissions standards, course content, and grading systems have been dominated by and responsive to white America, administered and taught primarily by whites, and reinforced by white classmates. Lacking what Glasgow calls a "critical mass," [7] black social work students have historically adapted to a white socialization process. Those blacks who succeeded did so because they were able to adapt to these circumstances; there was an unwritten law of color blindness for both black and white so that blackness added nothing. And many blacks did not survive; the social work profession had ample diagnostic terms to explain why not. As for the white students, their education was missing an important element, both formally and informally.

As the black percentage grows, the individual black has an alternative point of reference and self-comparison. Instead of defining himself only in terms of the white majority, he receives support from fellow blacks. An important additional element in this is the presence of black teachers. Among other things, the black student is less likely to lose his special interest in and concern for the plight of other blacks. In the early stages of group self-awareness, this common perception may be self-conscious, and those blacks who appear to stand aloof may be subject to hostility and even overt pressure to demonstrate group solidarity. As the minority comes to feel less threatened by the majority, this coercive tendency will probably lessen. When white faculty and students become upset about the apparent clannishness of blacks, they need to be aware that they are witnessing a mild expression of a very profound experience in the wider society, as blacks seek to work out a new relationship to the dominant majority—a relationship far more mature than the subservience that preceded it.

In the long run, are schools of social work to become houses divided, a kind of uneasy no-man's-land between competing groups? They are most likely to do that if the educating process itself is not influenced by the insight coming from the minority component. And both the traditional, clinically oriented old guard and the newer, academically oriented faculty members have difficulty in incorporating what blacks and other minorities have to offer into social work education. This may be especially true of the academicians, who have been steeped in "the" scientific tradition. The very skepticism with which they have been imbued can mislead them into believing that it is acultural skepticism.

What do black teachers and students bring to social work education that is distinctively black? There is a tendency for educators to view this in very concrete and narrow terms: they can tell the whites about life in the ghetto. That leads to social work's Catch-22: those blacks who grew up in middle-class homes and never lived in an inner-city slum presumably have nothing special to offer, but they are the ones most likely to get faculty appointment because of the traditional academic and professional expectations. Conversely, the welfare rights leader who lacks the academic credentials to become a faculty member is very popular as visiting lecturer.

But blacks of whatever social background do have much to contribute from their own life experience. Minorities characteristically are subject to the sharpest manifestations of societal pathologies affecting us all. Many blacks know the personal costs of rising above their beginnings. They have a special awareness of the foibles of the majority and of themselves. Living in a white-dominated world, blacks have had to learn to cope with whites. They thus tend to be sensitive to both societies. The white majority finds it easier to isolate itself from the minority and to view it from a distance in terms of flat stereotypes. Not all blacks are able or willing to articulate this sensitivity; but, particularly in recent years, the greater problem has been the whites' unreadiness to hear.

But the distinctive black contribution to social work education that is hardest for whites to grasp is that which involves thoughtways themselves. We know that knowledge and intellectual activity are never culture-free. German sociologists have had particular ways of working that were functionally related to the society that spawned them. And psychology today is different from psychology of another era in this country, not only because of the accumulation of knowledge in the interim but also in response to the present society.

So when white, academically oriented social work educators say that a black student cannot think conceptually, they are saying that his way of organizing his experience is not theirs. The tragedy is double, because not only is the black learner likely to be cast aside as inadequate; it also means that his white judges will not be able to learn from him.

This problem is not just one of narrowness and parochialism disguised as true reason. It is more serious than that, because black thought patterns have been molded out of a life experience much more germane to the problems of urban America than that of most white middle-class academicians. Not that one should thus romanticize street wisdom and ignore the richness that has been derived from scholarly inquiry. Instead, there needs to be a melding of the various strands that go to make up social work education today.

SECTION 4
CONCLUSION

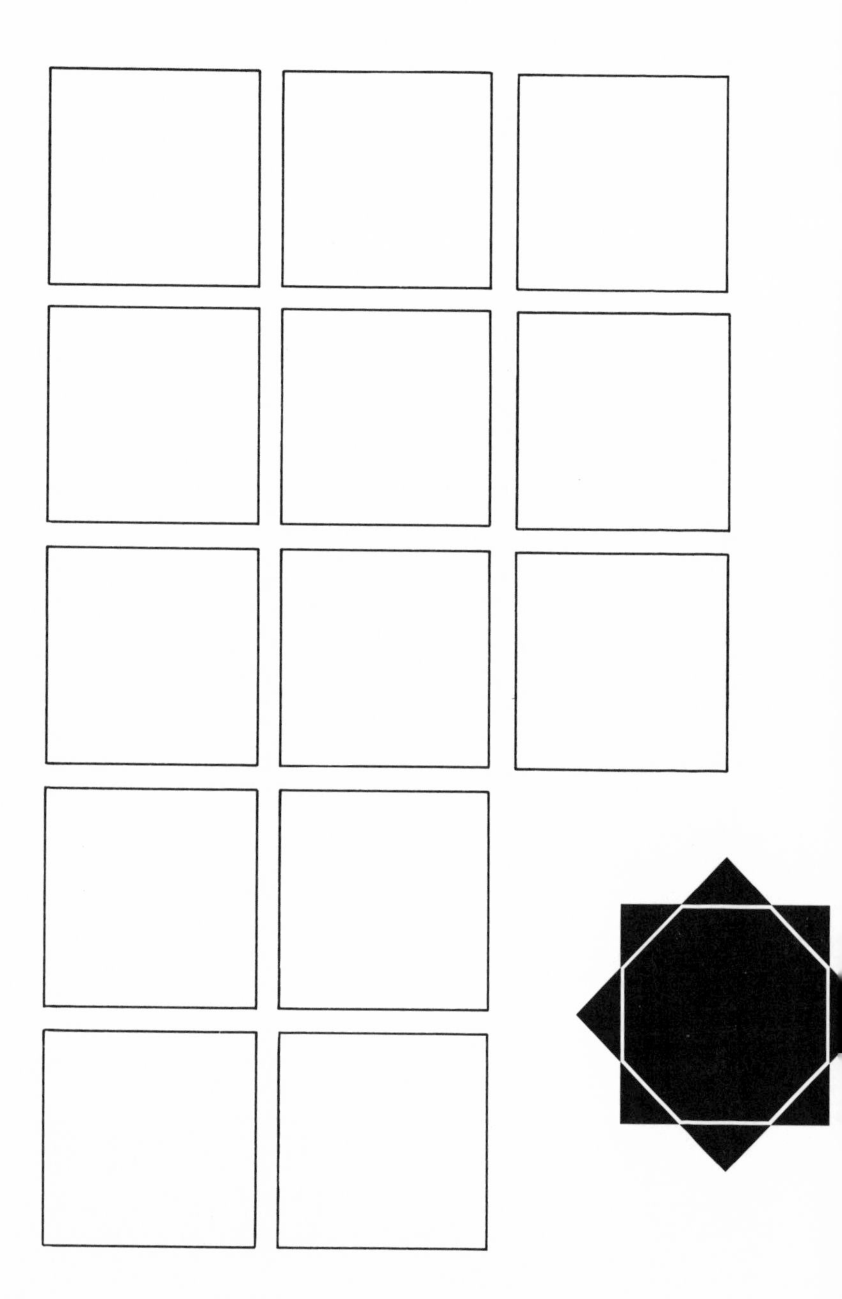

CHAPTER 9
FACING UP

Social work is a profession in crisis—and it should be clear from what has been said that this is a crisis of identity. In the past, social work has experienced institutional schizophrenia, its several parts going their own ways. Once it could do this and still pretend it was a single profession because of the looseness of its self-conception. But as the issues have sharpened in recent decades, it has become harder and harder to ignore the internal contradictions. Social work is one of those institutions that has had the function of keeping the society intact—of bridging the gaps between different elements in the nation and of repairing rents in the national fabric. And as the society has been plunged into turmoil and conflict, institutions such as social work have been under heavy stress.

Social work can no longer gloss over the differences within it. It is the time for making choices. We believe one option is completely out of the question—that of clinging to the part of social work that is dying. We mean the part of social work that has drifted farther and farther away from working with the poor and that has systematically excluded the poor from its ranks. The more affluent the clientele, the more respectable the professional. When this social worker does get involved with the poor he demonstrates his "trained incapacity" to respond effectively. He would like the poor to recede quietly into the background.

But the poor have *refused* to remain so quietly poor. They are visible, loud, threatening, and demanding, and they are reaching out for political power. The methods they are using are not methods learned from the social workers: confrontation, militancy, political awareness, and direct physical action are not really a part of the traditional social worker's methods; however, the poor have learned that these are the essential ways by which their voices are heard in the society.

It can be argued that social work has indirectly assisted in this process by developing a sense of dignity and self-worth in the poor. And, of course, it must be acknowledged that many social workers have been active in the welfare rights movements, have engaged in civil disobedience, and have even gone to jail on behalf of the poor. Several years ago this kind of activity would have been completely unthinkable for a social worker. But the profession as a whole has not moved that far. Only a handful of social workers have been involved in direction action, which remains distinctly outside the pale for the great majority of social work professionals.

While there has been considerable hand-wringing for years in professional social work circles about the inequities and the crass inhumanity of the public welfare system, it was only recently that any direct methods were advocated to bring about a fundamental change. For instance, it is a recent argument that welfare reform can be obtained only by guaranteeing that every person who is eligible for public assistance is placed on welfare rolls, and is not only given assistance but also receives the full benefits mandated by law. Costs, it has been argued, would skyrocket; the degrading system of public welfare would break down; and a more humane and appropriate system for the distribution of societal resources would replace it. But this type of direct action strikes at the system that helps create the problem; it has more in common with the early promise of social work than with the psychic interventions of Freud.

The ghetto is still new to many. In today's scene it is real, visible, and frightening. The black faces peering over its walls are not bubbling with love and gratitude for their white overlords. These people have bitter, deeply angry faces. Their fists are clenched and their eyes are hungry. Words can no longer serve to pacify; action is demanded—real action—immediate action —or else. . . .

The "or else" is often terror. It may be fire, burning, looting—rational or irrational violence. The city streets are no longer safe. Big doors, big locks, barking dogs, burglar alarms, more police, higher walls, more security—the middle class is being attacked.

As the ghetto overflows its walls and pours into middle- and upper-class streets, these poor will be new faces for the frightened people staring out of their comfortable, warm apartments. But these are by no means new faces for the social worker. The first social workers plodded the streets of slums and the ghetto. Aside from the residents of the ghetto themselves, no one was as aware of the grinding misery, the degrading numbness, and the naked hunger of the ghetto as the social worker. But to what end? In all the years that social workers have been plying their trade in the ghetto, what efforts have they made to change the conditions that have produced the ghetto? Where have they intervened—even unsuccessfully—to change those conditions that have produced the ghetto? Where have been their cries of rage and anguish? Now the ghetto's response to the ineffectiveness of the social worker has become increasingly threatening and menacing.

In New York City during the 1950's, the social worker from the Department of Welfare was always a welcome sight in the ghetto. The social worker was generally afforded a considerable degree of protection by the inhabitants. And why not? He carried with him the instrument for their survival, his "black book," a looseleaf folder that contained information about his clients—names, addresses, their rents, their incomes, and whatever they were entitled to. This black looseleaf book was prominently displayed by the worker while in the field: it was his passport to the ghetto.

Today the scene is strikingly different. The "black book" is no longer a protective badge; quite the contrary, it has become a symbol of enemy identification. As the uniformed police and firemen are today marked as agents of an oppressive regime, so is the social worker marked by his black book. Social workers today do not go out into the field. If absolutely necessary, they tend to go in pairs for protection. White social workers are not assigned to black ghettos. The black book remains completely out of sight. In the eyes of the ghetto residents, the social worker has changed from friend to enemy; he has become the target instead of the savior; he has become identified with the most repressive forces of the Establishment. He is no longer the giver but the denier, not the enabler but the preventer—the unloved social worker.

The rage now being directed at the social worker by the poor is largely deserved. Despite his good intentions and his carefully phrased concern for the plight of the poor, the social worker's actual response to conditions of poverty has been excessively feeble, if not sometimes dangerous. Working through a system that is niggardly and obsessively moralistic with the poor, the social worker in his treatment of poverty has become more concerned with justifying the denial of public funds than with finding more effective ways of using them to meet needs. He is caught in a vise between the rising costs of welfare and his own humanistic strivings. What could the social worker offer the poor but psychological understanding and placating words? Unable to stand the squeeze, most professional social workers have stayed away from fields such as public welfare. Outside of the massive welfare bureaucracies, only some local settlement houses and a scattering of small private agencies with limited resources and restrictive operating conditions have continued to struggle with the problems of poverty. In short, social work has done literally nothing about the conditions of the ghetto except for charitable tidbits and polysyllabic tokenism.

It is as if social workers did not even know that the poor were poor because they lacked money. If they were aware of this monumental simplicity, one would assume that the major thrust of the field would be to channel money to the poor—not to channel money to social workers to be funneled to the poor via services. Required courses in economic theory are not offered in social work schools; the distribution of resources in society is not a feature of the curriculum. A lead curtain is drawn over areas that have significant relevancy to the lives of the deprived masses. No economic alternatives to the existing system are proposed or pondered, and the existing system itself is not plumbed for its strengths and failings. The status quo is a given—a higher reality—not to be questioned but to be blindly accepted. It is not the social worker's arena.

By asking questions regarding the purpose of social work, by examining its current stance, its teaching, and its practice, it is hoped that the way may be paved for a more meaningful impact of the field on today's world. There is a value, and what is meaningful and relevant should be preserved. Its basic set of values; its subscription to the principles of self-determination and the dignity of the individual; and its role as enabler, advocate, and activist: these are important and necessary in today's social turbulence. Social work has made important contributions in many areas—areas in which the determining forces lie outside the individual and are the least subject to interventional movements and change. Aging and death, for example, are realities that are not subject to radical alterations, given man's knowledge to date. Social work is dealing with these problems; its working with the individuals and families concerned is highly praiseworthy. Similarly, its work with the blind, the physically handicapped, the diseased, and the mentally retarded, and its involvement with children in adoption and foster care, have been important and necessary. But as important as this work may be, it cannot be substituted for the essential purpose of the social work promise: the promotion of the welfare of mankind. These are but the fringes of the problem; social work has not directly faced its causes. Social work must be recognized more by its denial and its refusal to deal with the social realities and their effects on people, by its implicit agreement with the system to preserve the system, and by its overall denial of its eclectic nature, than by any listing of its good works. Just as it has failed the system, it has failed to meet the needs of the poor. It has reached for status and professional recognition, and it is being hanged now by its failure to translate its rhetoric into practice.

Clearly the key to social work's future does not lie in its recent past. The dissatisfaction with what it has become is pervasive—both inside and outside the field. Is this, then, the end of the road for a might-have-been profession? We reject that alternative as too costly for society, for from the beginning there has been in social work a vital and creative thread that is needed now more than ever. Social work must change and change drastically. The real question is what path it must follow if it is to carve out a viable and relevant future.

One view holds that a radical rebirth and reconception of social work is necessary if social work is to survive in the current scene in any meaningful way. The "if" is important, for even with radical overhaul there is little evidence that the profession has the wherewithal, the flexibility, or the machinery to deal with the overwhelming social changes around us. There is plenty of evidence to the contrary, and in this view the field appears ossified, confused, and increasingly controlled by its bureaucratization of practice and by the conservatism of its mentors. Whatever relief is in sight for the miserable in our society is coming not from professional social work but from other directions—directions not even thought of five years ago. One direction is through the poor themselves, from their growing understanding of their own political strength and the latent power inherent in their numbers. The other direction for change is truly novel—through the business community. Who would have thought that the business community—the bankers, the brokers, and the merchants—would start moving in where social work has failed, toward resolving the broad social problems of the day? Yet it is true. No, the business community has not suddenly gone altruistic. Such ventures are to protect business interests, but the public relations people, the bank presidents, and the corporation executives *are* currently meeting—without social workers, it may be added—to pool their expertise to deal with social problems.

Rather than addressing itself to these problems, social work continues to pursue the hollow path of professional acceptance. This pursuit has been the albatross of social work since the introduction of the Freudian tools, and it has led social work farther and farther from its avowed principles and goals. With every inch it has earned in acceptance, it has moved a mile from the needs and concerns of the people it was designed to serve. The new image of the social worker now being fostered is that of the manager—and who can deny the role of the manager in a managerial society? Not only are managerial concepts sterile, but even the words themselves sound false in the social worker's mouth. It is indeed ironic. Not only is psychiatry—the idol of social work—moving into the community that social workers have deserted; big business itself—the arch-enemy of humanistic principles—is moving into the cauldron of social injustice that social work in its finest hour has refused even to recognize.

The second view holds more hope for social work. While equally dissatisfied with what social work has become, it sees in recent developments within the profession the beginnings of a renaissance, a new professionalism. Even as vested interests try to divert these new thrusts into old, outworn channels and abort the drive for change, things have gone too far—it is too late to turn back.

Blacks, chicanos, and other minority Americans who are entering social work in ever-growing numbers will not allow the profession to turn back. The attempts to keep them in the service of the white majority may have worked when they represented only a relative handful of social workers, but they are now approaching the "critical mass"—both in the schools and in the field—that will allow them to exercise significant political leverage. We can see many of the halting movements toward social change in the professional establishment as directly related to this new force.

The Council on Social Work Education has legitimized the serious involvement of students in the business of shaping social work education and delegitimized the kind of clinical thought-control that used to dominate the schools. Having been socialized to a new and more independent role as professionals, graduates enter social agencies with a new sense of purpose.

Even the tenuousness of social work's relationship with some traditional sectors of the social welfare industry and outright rejection by fields once dominated by self-interested cadres of social work professionals can be a blessing in disguise, for it will force social work to seek out new relationships and a new image of itself.

This last may sound wishful and far-fetched. How can social work—at the nadir of its relations both with ghetto populations and with service systems that sought it out in the past—go anywhere from here? Has it not used up its options? Not quite. For one thing, there are fields that most social workers have shied away from in the past, but that offer fertile ground for a revolutionary mission. For example: corrections. Blacks and other minorities in our large prisons have come to see the political dimension of their plight; they need friends inside and outside the system who can form bridges between them and the Establishment, who can help translate the explosive potential they represent into meaningful gains. The Commissioner of Youth Corrections in Massachusetts, a psychiatric social worker by background, directed the abolition of juvenile correctional facilities in that state in one stroke, despite the misgivings of legislators and private citizens.[1] Meanwhile, increasing numbers of prisoner advocacy organizations are springing up around the country, in the business of defending prisoners' rights and getting a fair shake for those discharged from prison. When the corrections field beckons to social workers, the official beckoners aren't looking for revolutionaries; they want social workers who perform the old function of maintaining control. But the social worker as an institutional subversive must define a different and more vital kind of function.

Private industry is another arena that many social workers have avoided for fear of being used by a self-interested system—all the while letting themselves be used by other self-interested systems. But the industrial giants have tremendous control over the lives of all Americans: who gets hired and who gets laid off; the quality of life for everybody from the assembly line automatons inside the plant to the consumers outside; the mindless junk that children watch on the tube every Saturday morning; and the pollution of the environment. There are important jobs to be done—jobs right in line with what the new professional has to offer—in industry, in labor unions, in regulatory agencies, and in consumer rights organizations.

A field in which the *old* professionals have felt at home, but that turned off the newer breed, is marital and family counseling. The field has epitomized the preoccupation with the psyche that has given social work such a bad case of professional myopia; in the large public bureaucracy it has been a tool of social control of the poor. That is because the social workers in this field have neglected the political dimension of their work. But that dimension becomes paramount in such movements as women's lib. Women are the largest exploited "minority" group (they are actually in the majority) in our society. There is a vast range of tasks that need to be done and are completely in line with the new professionalism: consciousness-raising among housewives; political education and mobilization to help women develop the clout needed to assert their rights; and *men's* liberation—liberating husbands from the superiority complex that accounts for so many coronaries in the fifty- to sixty-year age group.

Everywhere there is a captive population, there is a need for the social-worker-as-revolutionary. Staying away from the "corrupting" influence of some of these settings will do no good; social workers have demonstrated over the years that you can be corrupted just about anywhere. As long as social workers were taught to identify with the agency, they had good reason to fear getting involved in punitive systems. But the institutional subversive is at his best in the organization that he *knows* has harmful potential, for then his guard is up.

This is the view of the reformer, the one who believes social work has the wherewithal *now* to begin to change the system, from inside as well as from outside. It is based on the belief that the vital spark *is* burning stronger and can point the way to a new professionalism, a professionalism with revolutionary potential.

These two views of social work lead to different prescriptions for its redemption. One is a radical redefinition of social work, calling for a basic rejection of professionalism in its conventional meaning and a totally different approach to social work education from what presently exists. The other is basically one of reform from within, capitalizing on present professional and educational structures instead of eliminating them.

This book does not answer the question "Which way?" It has sought to pose the question in sharp and clear terms. We leave it for our readers to pick up the challenge at that point.

APPENDIX
A PRIMER FOR CHANGE: HOW TO TURN A SERVICE SYSTEM AROUND

If there is a single basic message in what has been said up to this point, it is that there is no royal road to social change. It is hard work, often boring, and it requires intelligence. So this appendix does *not* present a neatly packaged training course. It simply offers fundamental steps for anybody intent on changing the way social institutions go about his business. We have referred to institutional subversives, but we do not necessarily mean subversion in the literal sense; that is, overthrowing or destroying institutions outright. In fact, through the application of the right tactics, one may even be said to be saving a system in spite of itself (assuming, of course, that the system is worth saving). Here are some basic principles, then, for turning an organization in a new direction.

PREPARE FOR THE WORST BY EXPECTING THE BEST.
That may sound like odd advice. No, we are not turning into Pollyannas. What we are suggesting is that you set up positive expectations—in yourself and in other people. If you assume that the system won't change, you will act accordingly. Morale will wilt easily, with every negative reaction simply confirming your worst fears. Pessimism is even more deadly for a group of allies who cannot afford faltering spirits.

Positive expectations also affect the tactics you employ with a system, as well as the system's response. When you go in believing people will agree with you, you are less likely to start in by blitzing your target and heaping unnecessary abuse on it—a sure way to force the system to reject your position. There is time enough for conflict tactics later on if the situation requires them. As for the response, by starting out with an implicit assumption that the target will agree with you, you impose your expectations on the target; this forces the target either to agree or initiate a negative response. If somebody is nasty toward us, we usually find little trouble in reacting in kind. But there is an inherent tendency not to be unpleasant with somebody who is being nice. And as any house-to-house salesman will tell you, each yes from the quarry makes the next yes a little easier. The additional advantage in starting off with positive expectations is that you convey your own feeling of confidence. A hostile entry is almost a sure sign of weakness.

Hard to believe? Are key decision-makers in organizations really that vulnerable? Yes, they *are* that vulnerable—more about that in a moment. And how do you *make* yourself feel confident? Understanding what has just been said, you may feel a little bit more confident already. But it also takes practice. You see, if you behave confidently, you will start a chain reaction; and as you realize some success, that will actually make you more confident. Psychologists are realizing that the relationship between attitudes and behavior is not the simple-minded notion we used to think it was: that of attitudes causing behavior. Behavior can also produce attitude changes—especially if it is successful behavior.

But reading it is not nearly as convincing as experiencing it firsthand. So try a few experiments. Here are some—you will think of others.

Experiment 1. Pick out a friend, a nice, understanding friend, and ask him or her a favor. Something more than you would commonly ask. Not an absurd favor, but still a thing that you might ordinarily expect the friend to refuse. (We won't try to say what—you know your friends better than we do.) Now stop a moment. Before broaching the subject, take yourself aside and tell yourself that the friend is going to say yes. After all, this is a friend who is generally disposed to please you. And especially if you convey a sense of confidence (you *are* deserving of it) and are nice about it (because you anticipate the friend is going to be nice), chances are the friend *will* agree. We leave you with the questions of whether you should tell your friend later what this was all about! He might feel he was being used. Actually it wasn't your friend you were using psychology on but yourself. You knew that, didn't you?

Experiment 2. Next, do the same thing with somebody who is not a nice, understanding friend. A sheer stranger is best for this. Perhaps you could volunteer to do canvassing for a worthy cause of some kind. Remember the positive approach; be confident that you can persuade the target. The canvassing has an added advantage; you will be approaching many people, some of whom will say yes and some of whom will say no. First of all, you should find that the initial feeling of confidence will improve your batting average. And, more important, you will learn that each rejection of your charm does not have to be a crushing experience. If face-to-face encounters of this kind are hard, start out with telephone canvassing and work up to the in-person kind. Incidentally, you should have no trouble finding opportunities of this sort; the world is full of worthy causes—from the March of Dimes to local political candidates. Needless to say, the cause should be one you really believe in; otherwise, the confidence wears a little thin.

Experiment 3. Pick out somebody who has authority over you or a person who intimidates you. Use the same routine. Make the proposal something the person could realistically agree to if he wished to. Yes, you are completely justified in asking the person to do it. Do not be discouraged if this attempt does not succeed. Try it a few times. Short of acceding outright to your request, the person should at least be put to some efforts to justify his refusal—evidence that you were able to force him to take the initiative in being negative.

LOOK FOR THE ACHILLES' HEELS IN THE SYSTEM.

It has them. The first step is to understand just how vulnerable most organizations are. The folklore about bureaucracies is that they never change. In reality, they are always adapting to changes around them and inside them—adjusting to pressures, even shifting to new tasks in order to survive. There is no magic in this. Systems involve people who have a stake in doing things in the same way and in being able to predict what the people around them will do. But, fortunately, people's interests are changing and are often in conflict, inside and outside the system. So there is always a certain amount of yeast in any organization.

Any social welfare system is a finely tuned balance of forces. In order to operate, it needs three kinds of resources: money, staff, and clientele. The sources of these three factors have potential leverage on the system because they can withhold the needed resources. Some of these kinds of leverage are more obvious than others. We all know what happens if the funds dry up: the organization goes out of business. If the staff withdraws its labor—as in a strike—this, too, can halt operations, at least temporarily.

What is less commonly recognized is the potential leverage of the clients; if they stop using the agency in question it has no basis for going after funds. When public assistance programs in the late 1960's and early 1970's stopped requiring that people accept counseling in order to receive money, it created a crisis for the social workers doing the counseling, for their clients voted no with their feet in large numbers.

There is one other kind of support organizations need: social sanction. Either by law or by common public agreement, the society has to approve of the social welfare system if it is to continue functioning. And in particular there has to be approval by the people who control those three kinds of resources—government sponsors and congressional appropriations committees; professional associations; professional schools and labor unions; and clients. When clients come together in organizations such as welfare rights groups, they can express their approval or disapproval in a way that has an impact on the system.

Inside the organization, all these resources and sanctions get translated into the operation of the program through an intricate system of work roles, relationships among people, and mechanisms for reinforcing desired behavior. If one understands the fact that the organization's ultimate purpose is to use people in order to keep itself functioning, to keep those essential resources flowing, it is possible to make sense out of the welter of activity that goes on inside.

Where are the Achilles' heels? At every one of those points where the system depends upon somebody for resources or sanction *and* points inside, the system must induce people to help it operate—money sources (can it demonstrate that it is a worthwhile investment?), professional bodies (is it considered professional and therefore a good place to work?), its own staff, etc.

One of the misunderstood mechanisms for inducing people to behave the way the system wants them to is authority. According to the conventional wisdom, somebody at the top wields unfettered authority over those below. In actuality, authority flows from the bottom as much as it does from the top. It works this way: effective authority requires somebody who gives the orders and somebody who follows the orders. If the first person gives the orders and the second person does not follow them, you do not have effective authority. All right, you may say, then the first person cracks the whip. But excessive whip-cracking demonstrates that the first person does not have effective authority, so people at the top are usually very sparing in how much they resort to this kind of direct coercion.

Why does the boss check up on what his subordinates are doing and saying? To enforce his orders if they disobey, right? Not so much for that as in order to know what orders *will* be obeyed. The secret of authority: never give an order that the subordinates will not carry out.

How is this useful as a source of leverage? If subordinate staff and clients fail to follow the rules often enough, then those in authority have one of three choices: (1) punish the offenders (remember, to do that too often is a sign of weakness); (2) admit that one does not have authority; or (3) change the rules. And more times than people are willing to admit, it is actually the last of these that organizational hierarchies choose.

Since the Achilles' heels of systems are so important to the strategies of change, we will return to these from time to time. But for now we will turn to some more experiments.

Experiment 4. Using the kinds of factors that have been discussed in this section, do a careful analysis of a particular social welfare agency. If you are employed in one, that would be a good specimen because you are already familiar with many aspects of its operation. But you may find yourself looking at some old assumptions in a different light. Remember that we are talking about things that apply in one way or another to all organizations. Yes, that poised and forbidding character in the inner office has to walk tightropes daily in order to keep those necessary resources flowing and to maintain authority in the organization. One of the reasons it looks so easy is that everybody else in the shop is helping him maintain it. You may notice, for instance, that staff colleagues are normally one of the greatest regulating forces within an organization. Watch to see what they do if a newcomer to the organization expresses a "deviant" idea. More likely than not, it is they and not the boss who bring the person back in line by persuasion or, if necessary, isolation.

When you feel you have a good sense of what makes the organization tick, think of ways in which this nice, smooth process has been disrupted in the past or might be in the future. As you look at any organization, its Achilles' heels should become pretty evident.

Experiment 5. Think of some current practice within the organization that you would like to see changed. Make it a large enough change to cause real reverberations and require real internal adjustments, but also one that the organization is reasonably capable of making. And it should be a change that you believe the organization actually ought to make. The more conviction you have, the better. Next, propose it to anybody inside the system who you think would be an appropriate audience. Then watch to see what happens. If you have selected the right kind of change, the organization should start reacting. You should begin to see resistance. If the response is too bland, it perhaps means nobody is taking your proposal seriously. Press your idea until people *do* take it seriously. How does the system deal with this irritant? This will tell you something about how the organization copes with other internal disturbances.

Experiment 6. Do the same thing, only this time choose a change that involves modifications in those external relations with the sources of money, staff, clientele, and sanction. For example, it may require more money in order to accomplish the change, a different mandate from a government body, changes in the composition of the clientele, etc. You may find, incidentally, that this is not the best organization for achieving the desired goals and it ought to be replaced. All right, how would you bring that about?

Again, if the system's relationships with outside resources were threatened or disrupted, how would the system seek to regain its equilibrium?

KNOW MORE THAN THE SYSTEM DOES.

You already know many of the strengths and weaknesses of the system *in general*. What you need to do now is become the expert regarding a specific kind of change. Since it is impossible to know everything about everything, you have to choose a place to focus your attention. Maybe it is a set of requirements for receiving the services of the agency—rules that tend to weed out many people who need the service. Or it may be the way the intake staff behaves toward applicants, in violation of the intent of the organization. Perhaps hospital patients get caught in the middle of a conflict between two factions in the staff. Or maybe in order to keep on receiving the benefits (public assistance), a client has to behave in certain ways—ways that have nothing to do with his need for the benefits. Or inmates in a training school are subjected to brutal treatment for minor infractions.

Begin by giving the organization the benefit of the doubt. Does that sound like upside-down thinking? No, we are not suggesting ignoring the problem. What we are doing is telling you to assume the burden of proof. This will force you to gather the necessary evidence to support your claims that the organization is wrong. And this is exactly what you will have to do if anybody is going to listen to you. This is the same burden that a prosecuting attorney takes on when he accuses somebody of a crime. In this case, the organization is presumed innocent—so now go out and get the evidence to make your case. If clients or other community people are complaining to you, then make them share the burden of proof. The agency is unfair? Unfair how? How does a person know this? Can the agency change the situation, or is this something a legislative body has imposed on it? What would the complainant like to see happen? Does he reasonably expect that it could? One has to be careful not to come off sounding like an apologist for the system or to scare off the complainant. You can explain why you are asking these questions. If it is too threatening, you might say, "All right, suppose the director asks me. . . ."

If you are the only one who is complaining, put yourself through this kind of cross-examination. Make it just as pointed and specific as you can. That way you will make sure of getting solid evidence, and you will be in a very strong position when you go up against the system and its representatives.

When looking for evidence, think of people in and around the organization who can be trusted to give accurate information. Don't be swept along by things that you want to hear. Question those sources very closely. As you pursue the problem and its causes, and the changes you want to see take place, you may find that you need to consult the state laws, information on file in other agencies, old newspaper clippings in the library, etc.

Aside from the case itself, you need to understand who in or out of the organization can make the key decisions that will bring about the change. And you need to work out a basic change-strategy in your mind. It is impossible to spell out all the complexities of bureaucratic life and political institutions here. But at least you should direct your attention to the relevant questions. Do you remember the old problem of the strategy for all occasions? Don't get trapped in a single approach—among other things you will make yourself so predictable that potential allies will get bored and the opposition be waiting for you. Neither should your strategy be helter-skelter, based on the impulse of the moment. Instead, your strategy should be focused on the specific target you have selected.

As your strategy begins to take shape, you will identify key individuals and groups whom you need to move to action. Think carefully about their interests and the arguments that will appeal to them. Put yourself in their place. What tough questions will they ask you? How will you answer them? Chances are you will be much tougher on yourself in this kind of shadowboxing than the actual people ever will be.

As you build your case, develop your strategy, and think out your appeal to key people, you are also becoming an expert. It is not that you are any smarter than the people you are dealing with, but you are focused on the specific kind of subject-matter. They are most likely preoccupied with other things. In fact, you will find that apathy is a far greater enemy of your efforts than outright opposition. Is it hard to believe that you will know more than the organization? A few years ago, welfare clients armed themselves with knowledge of the welfare laws—to the point where they knew more than the people carrying them out.

A warning: it is exciting to score points in a debate. It will be tempting to show up the welfare director or the hospital administrator, to show that you know more than they do. As a *general* thing, this should be avoided. You may simply drive the person into a corner where he has to say no to save face. There are exceptions to this general rule: for instance, you may be able to intimidate a staff person if you show that you know more than he does, with the result that he will retreat rather than show his ignorance. Or if there is a "swing" group of citizens, whose loyalties might go either way, you may want to show them that your side is a better bet than the other side. As with anything, though, you gauge your approach by your assessment of what is needed.

Experiment 7. Select any facet of the work of the system. For instance, if it carries on health care activities, take a health problem with which the agency purports to deal. If in housing, you might focus on the laws dealing with housing. Spend a few days finding out everything you can about the subject—from people in the organization, the public library, outside experts, etc. Important: do not spend more than a few days' time, tucked in around all your other activities. You should discover that you will come to know a surprising amount about the subject in a very short time. The secret is concentration on that subject—immersion in it.

Experiment 8. Using what you have learned, talk with people considered somewhat expert on the subject. Listen closely. Try to find discrepancies between what they say and what other authoritative sources say. When you find such differences, raise them with the person. Press him to support his side of the case—say, as to what ought to be done about the problem. As you do, collect his arguments; then use these when you talk with somebody with a different viewpoint. You should now make two additional discoveries: how quickly you come to be viewed by others as knowing a lot about the subject (the further outside your field the better); and how little the so-called experts actually know when they are pressed with searching questions.

Experiment 9. Select a problem in the way the

agency operates (e.g., abusive practices with clients). Using the previous techniques, learn all you can about the practices—why they occur, their effects on the work of the organization and on the people they claim to serve. What has been tried elsewhere to deal with such practices? As you build up your store of information, begin to put together the case against the continuation of the practice. As an added help, play devil's advocate with yourself and with a friend. Who can change the practice? Who or what influences the person or persons who can make the key changes? Develop your strategy for changing things. As you think of people you would involve, consider how you would make use of their attitudes and interests to persuade them.

WHAT MAKES PEOPLE ACT?

The foregoing may suggest that people do things because of reasoned arguments. In part they do, but it would be naïve to suggest that that is all or even the most important part of what moves people. A person does what his own private calculus tells him will further his interests, and he avoids doing things that will harm his interests. It does not have to be all selfish motives —his interests may well be the public interest.

A way of thinking about this is in terms of costs and benefits. Once you have determined who is your target, think about the things that he or she considers costs or benefits. A benefit might be monetary rewards, social recognition, or peaceful staff relations. A cost might be disruption of the agency's operations. This, of course, is the whole point of a strike. Later on we discuss some specific ways of increasing or decreasing costs and benefits. But first you have to face a hard reality: you do not have a great deal of economic and political resources—the usual tools for manipulating costs and benefits. So you need allies. That is what the next section is all about.

LOOK FOR FRIENDS.

You will need them if you take system change seriously—especially if you are part of the system. This may be the most important step of all. Allies multiply your impact manyfold. They also are useful—if they stick together—when the going gets rough (e.g., somebody decides to retaliate against you). There is a third way in which allies help—one you might not think of immediately: they give you moral support and help you maintain your conviction about what you are doing. A person operating alone can begin to have self-doubts if everybody he comes in contact with tells him he is crazy. Social workers have a well-developed vocabulary for telling colleagues that they are crazy—in a nice way, of course. You can avoid this erosion of confidence if you have a circle of colleagues who share the same view you have. Such alliances don't just happen spontaneously, but they can be cultivated. Chances are that many people feel the way you feel. You will need to smoke them out; as you let your own agenda become known to people who seem to be trustworthy, they will be emboldened to reciprocate.

On specific issues, do not be too quick to write off the people with whom you ordinarily have little in common. You may find "strange bedfellows" becoming valued allies. This suggests, incidentally, that the great pastimes of gratuitously insulting people over thirty, people who clip their hair short, people who vote Republican, etc., are expensive luxuries. You cannot afford that kind of fun if you are serious about changing things. It is one thing to be co-opted and to pander to the Establishment reactionaries; it is quite another to use them. Of course, one has to be careful as to how he himself is being used and keep his eye on the target. There may be times, however, when strategy dictates sounding off at the opposition—for instance, when you are trying to mobilize a community group to carry out an action.

When looking for friends, be sure to include those both inside and outside the system. Probably the most powerful leverage on any system is that brought simultaneously from inside *and* outside. Labor unions that have the support of other unions and an international parent body are in the strongest position to deal with management. During the 1960's, welfare rights groups often had the active help of workers inside the welfare system who fed them key information, raised appropriate issues within the staff, etc. Particularly valuable are those outside friends who can influence the flow of funds, staff, and clientele into the system. Probably the single most important factor in whether a dissident group can survive is its internal solidarity. Organizations have their own weapons for weakening such groups and thus fomenting jealousy within the group: manipulating rewards, making it difficult to schedule meetings, or openly threatening retaliation, for example.

Experiment 10. Make a systematic analysis of potential allies in relation to the problem or proposal in Experiment 9. Make a chart like the one below. (You need to do it in relation to this problem, because just as there is no strategy for all occasions, there are people who will support you on one issue but not another.)

Now approach some people in each of those six cells and discuss the problem or proposal with them. If you get verbal agreement, try to find out how committed the person would be: would he or she be willing to work on the problem? If the person is neutral, see if you can

Chart 1
Analysis of Potential Allies

	Inside the System	Outside the System
Sure bets; you are confident they would support you		
Neutral or unpredictable		
You would expect them to be opposed to you on this issue		

generate some interest. If the person is opposed, see if you can deal with the opposing arguments.

You should be making another important discovery: you have to revise your original assumptions. You probably have more potential allies than you thought you did, and you may have found that some people you were sure of would fade away at the first frown of the opposition.

Experiment 11. Try to bring together a group of "sure bets" in your revised listing, to discuss ways of actually working on the problem together. Keep it ad hoc—they are coming together to work on this problem—not forming a friendship club. While the ideal group would combine people from inside and outside the system, you need to exercise judgment. Will it be awkward for the insiders to share their concern with outsiders? If so, you may want to work with them separately. Or to start with you may want to limit it to insiders—in order to keep the level of escalation at a minimum with the option of escalating later.

MATTERS OF STRATEGY.

It is obvious from everything that has been said up to now that tactics will vary widely, depending on the problem, your assessment of the system, and the kind of alliance you are able to put together. But here are general principles that may help you to think about specific strategies you should employ.

To polarize or depolarize? Is it wisest to seek a confrontation between those who want the change and those who oppose it? Think this one through carefully. If you start low-key and consensus-oriented, you can still reserve the option to draw the lines tighter and become more aggressive later on. Meanwhile, you avoid forcing the opposition into a corner prematurely, thus hardening the resistance unnecessarily. This low-key approach also appears more reasonable to potential allies who are not directly involved in the situation, so if the crunch comes later, the opposition must share the responsibility for the crisis.

You must weigh these considerations against the risks involved in a long-drawn-out process, which can be misunderstood by some allies as foot-dragging on your part. It may also suggest to the opposition that the issue need not be taken seriously. One cardinal principle: be leery of making threats you cannot back up. This is where it is important to assess how reliable your allies will be if things get difficult. A useful tactic is the *threat* of confrontation—best made implicitly instead of explicitly, so you don't need to back down later on.

Making it hard to say no and easy to say yes. Unless you are really out to demonstrate that the system itself is too far gone to try to salvage it (in which case you had better have a conception of what should replace the system and also be well reinforced for a tough fight), your objective is to get the system to make the changes you are after. The principle stated above has two parts. The first is to make it as difficult as possible to refuse the demand. A reasonable demand, well documented, is one means of doing this. The threat of negative consequences in the case of resistance is another. The target has to ask itself: what are the costs of *not* complying with the demand? This is one place where gradual escalation can be an effective tactic: at each point the opponent will find it easier to concede than to risk the next round of action. In other words, there is something to be gained from agreeing.

Finally, there is the approach known as slicing the salami. One redefines the situation by simply making minor changes in what one is doing, setting a new precedent and creating a new status quo. These thin salami slices add up to significant changes after a time. This tactic amounts to making judicious use of the fait accompli. Its power lies in the fact that people in authority are hesitant to make an issue over a minor incident. It forces the initiative for taking an issue onto the target system instead of onto the innovator.

As for making it easy to say yes, this is a very important but very little understood tool. The system must justify to itself the things it is doing, as well as justifying them to key constituencies. The change agent needs to help the system develop the justification for making concessions; in some ways, this can be a more potent weapon than raising the costs of saying no—just as the reasonableness of the demands weakens the justification for refusing to make them. In some instances, one can actually supply one's opponent with arguments that he can use with his own allies in rationalizing his actions.

A related tactic is allowing the opponent not to know. In one public welfare department a few years ago, the director was required to pass along to his staff an edict that would have made it hard for elderly recipients to get medical care. His staff, concerned about their elderly clients, found a way of getting around the ruling by careful use of rule-breaking tactics. Later on the edict was lifted. Two young staff members confessed to the director that they had failed to comply with his earlier directive. His reply was, "I suspected what you guys were doing—half of the staff was probably doing the same thing. If I had to admit I knew officially, I would have had to stop you!"

And then there is the need for those seeking change to pose demands with which the system can realistically comply; this is making it *possible* to say yes. One does not ask the welfare department to end poverty or a human relations commission to end prejudice. You need to assess whether the demands are wrong or whether you are after the wrong target system. This does not mean that you never go after a system that is not the ultimate cause of the problem. A local agency, feeling pressure from a client group, may in turn put pressure on its state or federal counterpart to make the necessary changes that would allow it to say yes.

But there is really only one way to start, and that is—to start. Injustices abound, and you should have no trouble finding targets for your efforts. Remember that it is real people who are being deprived of their rights, abused, and dehumanized. That should make you approach the matter of social change thoughtfully and soberly. But it should also make you begin *now*. Remember: if you wait for the "big" issue, you may find it has already happened. Don't put off until tomorrow what you will probably put off then, too.

CHAPTER 1

[1] For a description of what has happened in one characteristic field, child guidance, from a source which is not unsympathetic, see *Encyclopedia of Social Work* (New York: National Association of Social Workers, 1971), Vol. 1, p. 824. See also Richard A. Cloward and Irwin Epstein, "Private Social Welfare's Disengagement from the Poor: The Case of Family Adjustment Agencies," in *Social Welfare Institutions,* ed. Mayer N. Zald (New York: Wiley, 1965), pp. 623–644.

[2] Deborah Golden, Arnulf M. Pins, and Wyatt Jones, *Students in Schools of Social Work* (New York: Council on Social Work Education, 1972), pp. 45f.

[3] See *Closing the Gap . . . in Social Work Manpower* (Washington, D.C.: U.S. Department of Health, Education, and Welfare, 1965).

[4] See George Brager and Sherman Barr, "Perceptions and Reality, the Poor Man's View of Social Services," in *Community Action Against Poverty,* ed. George Brager and Francis P. Purcell (New Haven, Conn.: College and University Press, 1967), pp. 72–82. For a graphic picture of the fear and tension which social workers experience when exposed to the anger and resentment of the poor, see Sol Stern, "Down and Out in New York," *The New York Times Magazine* (October 22, 1972), pp. 46–66.

[5] James O. S. Huntington, "Philanthropy—Its Success and Failure," in *Philanthropy and Social Progress* (New York: Thomas Y. Crowell, 1893), p. 102.

[6] David Soyer, "Reaching Problem Families Through Settlement-Based Casework," *Social Work,* 6(2), July, 1961, 36.

CHAPTER 2

[1] Arnulf M. Pins, "Changes in Social Work Education and Their Implications for Practice," *Social Work,* 16(2), April, 1971, 10.

[2] The convergence is so notable, in fact, that it has led one group of writers to suggest the emergence of a new profession made up of psychoanalysts, psychiatrists, clinical psychologists, and psychiatric social workers. See William E. Henry, John H. Sims, and S. Lee Spray, *The Fifth Profession* (San Francisco: Jossey-Bass, 1971).

[3] For background on the evolution of the field from charity to counseling, see Frank J. Bruno, *Trends in Social Work* (New York:

Columbia University Press, 1948); Nathan Cohen, *Social Work in the American Tradition* (New York: Dryden Press, 1958); and Roy Lubove, *The Professional Altruist* (Cambridge, Mass.: Harvard University Press, 1965).

[4] Harold L. Wilensky and Charles N. Lebeaux, *Industrial Society and Social Welfare* (rev. ed.; New York: Free Press, 1965), p. 270.

[5] *Encyclopedia of Social Work* (New York: National Association of Social Workers, 1971), Vol. 2, p. 1583.

[6] *Social Security Bulletin,* 35(7), July, 1972, 37.

[7] *Social Security Bulletin,* 35(5), May, 1972, 49, 55.

[8] See Ida C. Merriam, "Social Welfare Expenditures, 1967–68," *Social Security Bulletin,* 31(12), December, 1968, 14–27; and *Encyclopedia of Social Work, op. cit.,* pp. 1584–1588.

[9] See Willard C. Richan, "New Curriculum Policy Statement: The Problem of Professional Cohesion," *Journal of Education for Social Work,* 7(2), Spring, 1971, 55–60.

CHAPTER 4

[1] Unless otherwise indicated, all figures in this chapter are from *Statistics on Social Work Education* (New York: Council on Social Work Education, 1970).

[2] Deborah Golden, Arnulf M. Pins, and Wyatt Jones, *Students in Schools of Social Work* (New York: Council on Social Work Education, 1972), p. 17.

[3] *Facts* (New York: Community Service Society of New York, undated bulletin).

[4] *New Directions for CSS* (New York: Community Service Society of New York, 1971). Bulletin 704.

[5] *Ibid.*

[6] *Ibid.*

[7] *Ibid.*

[8] Letter from Robert H. Mulreany, May 6, 1971.

[9] Robert Shockley, "Specialist," in *Contact,* ed. Noel Keyes (New York: Paperback Library, 1963).

[10] Ivan Illich, *Deschooling Society* (New York: Harper & Row, 1970, 1971).

[11] Harry Specht, "The Deprofessionalization of Social Work," *Social Work,* 17(2), March, 1972.

[12] Emmanuel Hallowitz, "Innovations in Hospital Social Work," *Social Work,* 13(4), July, 1972.

CHAPTER 5

[1] John G. Hill and Ralph Ormsby, "The Philadelphia Cost Study," *Social Work Journal,* 34, October, 1953, 168.

[2] Scott Briar, "The Casework Predicament," *Social Work,* 13(1), January, 1968, 7. This article is strongly recommended in view of its incisive critique of casework as a method.

[3] *Ibid.*

CHAPTER 6

[1] Letter to the Editor, *The Social Service Review,* 38(1), March, 1964, 99f.

[2] *Ibid.*

[3] "Notes and Comments," *The Social Service Review,* 41(3), September, 1967, 308.

[4] "Berkan Appealing Dismissal as County Director, May Go to State Court," *NASW News,* 17(5), August–September, 1972, 4.

[5] See Gerald R. Wheeler, "America's New Street People: Implications for Human Services," *Social Work,* 16(3), July, 1971, 19–24. See also Ellen Dunbar and Howard Jackson, "Free Clinics for Young People," *Social Work,* 17(5), September, 1972, 27–34.

[6] See Nelly A. Peissachowitz and Anne R. Sarcka, "Social Action Groups in a Mental Health Program," in *Human Services and Social Work Responsibility,* ed. Willard C. Richan (New York: National Association of Social Workers, 1969), pp. 75–89.

[7] Interview with Philip Carter of CRLA Senior Citizens' Project, and project materials.

[8] "Report of Observation in Jackson and Hinds County, Mississippi, Re: The Schwerner Fund Project" (Unpublished memorandum; National Association of Social Workers, 1967).

[9] Albert Deutsch, *The Mentally Ill in America* (2nd ed. rev.; New York: Columbia University Press, 1949), pp. 158ff.

[10] See Arthur M. Schlesinger, Jr., *The Politics of Upheaval* (Boston: Houghton Mifflin, 1960), pp. 343–361. See also *Frontiers of Human Welfare* (New York: Community Service Society, 1948), pp. 54f.

CHAPTER 7

[1] Stanley Milgram, "Some Conditions of Obedience and Disobedience to Authority," *Human Relations,* 18(1), 1965, 57–76.

[2] See Andrew J. Billingsley, "Bureaucratic and Professional Orientation Patterns in Social Casework," *The Social Service Review,* 38(4), December, 1964, 400–407. See also Herman Piven, "Professionalism and Organizational Structure: Training and Agency Variables in Relation to Practitioner Orientation and Practice" (Unpublished doctoral dissertation, Columbia University, 1961).

[3] "Agency Exonerated by Commission on Complaint Filed by Member," *Personnel Information,* 5(6), November, 1962, 26.

[4] The Association's Ad Hoc Committee on Advocacy based its enunciation of this policy on the very language used in the case of Mrs. B—"I regard as my primary obligation the welfare of the individual or group served. . . ." This policy was accepted in principle by the NASW Board of Directors. See Ad Hoc Committee on Advocacy, "The Social Worker as Advocate: Champion of Social Victims," *Social Work,* 14(2), April, 1969, 16–22.

CHAPTER 8

[1] For a view of behavioral modification which is more sanguine, see Edward J. Thomas, "Behavioral Modification and Casework," in *Theories of Social Casework* (Chicago: University of Chicago Press, 1970), pp. 181–218.

[2] For an exploration of the problem and some suggested ways of protecting against violation of clients' civil rights, see John H. Noble, Jr., "Protecting the Public's Privacy in Computerized Health and Welfare Information Systems," *Social Work,* 16(1), January, 1971, 35–41.

[3] See Scott Briar, "The Casework Predicament," *Social Work,* 13(1), January, 1968, 5–11; and Henry J. Meyer, Edgar F. Borgatta, and Wyatt Jones, *Girls at Vocational High* (New York: Russell Sage Foundation, 1965).

[4] Between 1960 and 1966, the percentage of black students in entering classes in graduate programs actually declined, even as the field sought to recruit more minority students. See Deborah Golden, Arnulf M. Pins, and Wyatt Jones, *Students in Schools of Social Work* (New York: Council on Social Work Education, 1972), p. 12.

[5] See Douglas Glasgow, "The Black Thrust for Vitality: The Impact on Social Work Education," *Journal of Education for Social Work,* 7(2), Spring, 1971, 9–18.

[6] As quoted in Glasgow, *op. cit.* See also Morton Teicher, "Reverse Discrimination," *Social Work,* 17(6), November, 1972, 3–4.

[7] *Ibid.*

CHAPTER 9

[1] Bill Kovach, "Massachusetts Reforms to Doom Youth Prisons," *The New York Times* (January 31, 1972), p. 1.

Willard C. Richan was a radio news editor, a junior high school teacher and an aide in psychiatric wards before becoming a social worker. His career has taken him from the back roads of rural Wisconsin as a child welfare worker to the streets of Manhattan as a community center director. He received both his master's and doctoral degrees from the Columbia University School of Social Work. For the last twelve years he has been a social work educator and is now Associate Dean of the Temple University School of Social Administration. He has written on such diverse subjects as de facto school segregation and nonprofessionals in the human services.

Allan R. Mendelsohn was born in Brooklyn and received his B.A. degree from Brooklyn College. He received an M.A. degree in psychology from the New School of Social Research and an M.S.W. from the New York University School of Social Work. Mr. Mendelsohn worked for the New York City Department of Welfare as a social investigator and for the Bureau of Child Welfare. After receiving his M.S.W. he worked with delinquent youth for the New York State Department of Social Welfare. He was a supervisor at Mobilization for Youth, a community out-reach program, and an administrator at the Hawthorne Cedar Knolls School—a residential treatment setting for emotionally disturbed children. In recent years he has been a field instructor for the Hunter College School of Social Work and is now Assistant Professor of Field Work at the Columbia University School of Social Work.